FIDUCIARY

"If you are an investor looking to learn how to find, hire, and establish an aligned and trusted relationship with a fee-only wealth advisor, *Fiduciary* provides the answers in simple, easy-to-understand terms. Look no further."

—LARRY SWEDROE, author of *The Only Guide to a Winning Investment Strategy You'll Ever Need* and *Enrich Your Future*

"One of the standout features of *Fiduciary* is its accessibility. Instead of drowning readers in complex financial jargon, Ryan presents information in a clear and concise manner, making it easy for individuals at any level of financial literacy to grasp the concepts discussed. Whether you're just starting out on your financial journey or looking to reassess your current advisor relationship, this book offers practical advice, actionable steps, and invaluable insights to help you make the best decision for your financial future. It's a must-read for anyone seeking to secure their financial well-being."

GEOFFREY I. KANNER, CFP®, Kanner Financial Services LLC

"Ryan does a great job explaining the landscape of the financial advisory industry, detailing how best to find an advisor, discussing what to expect from a good advisory engagement, and providing insight into what a successful relationship and outcome should look like. I highly recommend this book to anyone who's interested in learning more about the financial advisory world and how to make a better-informed decision about finding their own advisor."

—ANDY PANKO, CFP® and owner of Tenon Financial

"Finding an advisor who always puts clients before themselves is the definition of a fiduciary, and Ryan explains to readers the importance of understanding this distinction. As an investor or person saving for retirement or something else, you owe it to yourself to know who is on your side and who may not be. This book can be a valuable tool in that endeavor."

—STEVEN D. LOCKSHIN, principal at AdvicePeriod
and author of *Get Wise to Your Advisor*

"Being a fiduciary is more than just a job, it's a responsibility to always act in the best interest of others. Ryan's book brilliantly captures the essence of what it means to be a fiduciary and is a must-read for anyone in the financial industry. Highly recommended!"

—MICHAEL COLLINS, CFA,
founder and CEO of WinCap Financial

"*Fiduciary* is a complete guide to understanding the investment advisory and financial planning industry. Ryan wrote this book in a way that the reader can directly and immediately apply his guidance to find, vet, and choose an advisor. He even covers how to "keep your advisor honest" along the way. I would recommend this book to anyone looking to understand the need for, find, and engage a competent fiduciary financial advisor."

—SHAUN M. JONES, CFS, CFP®, president of Jones Fiduciary
Wealth Management and author of *Unbrainwashed Investing*

FIDUCIARY

FIDUCIARY

How *to* Find,
Hire, *and* Establish
an Aligned *and*
Trusted Partnership
with a
Fee-Only
Financial Advisor

Ryan R. Morrissey

BOULDER KNOLL BOOKS

Published 2024
Printed in the United States of America
Hardcover ISBN: 979-8-9901238-0-9
Paperback ISBN: 979-8-9901238-1-6
Alt Paperback ISBN: 979-8-9901238-3-0
Ebook ISBN: 979-8-9901238-2-3
Library of Congress Control Number: 2024903733

Boulder Knoll Books
North Haven, CT
boulderknollbooks@gmail.com

Editing and book design by Stacey Aaronson

The information provided in this book is for informational purposes only and is not intended to be a source of advice or analysis with respect to the material presented. The information and/or documents contained in this book do not constitute legal or financial advice and should never be used without first consulting with a financial professional to determine what may be best for your individual needs. The publisher and the author do not make any guarantee or other promise as to any results that may be obtained from using the content of this book. You should never make any investment decision without first consulting with your own financial advisor and conducting your own research and due diligence. To the maximum extent permitted by law, the publisher and the author disclaim any and all liability in the event any information, commentary, analysis, opinions, advice and/or recommendations contained in this book prove to be inaccurate, incomplete or unreliable, or result in any investment or other losses.

I dedicate this book to my beautiful wife, Tiffany.
You are one in a billion and I'm lucky to have your amazing
inspiration in my life

To my children, Ryan and Emilia, who light up my life,
and my parents for instilling in me the values of hard work
and fairness

1. fi . du . ci . ary, *adjective*

of, or relating to, or involving a
confidence or trust: such as

a   : held or founded in trust or
        confidence

// *a fiduciary relationship*

b   : holding in trust

2. fi . du . ci . ary, *noun*

one that holds a fiduciary relation
or acts in a fiduciary capacity

TABLE OF CONTENTS

I

INTRODUCTION

———◦———

U ntil the golf bug bit me when I was a freshman in high school, I'd never had a reason to earn a large sum of money. Growing up, if there was something my brother or I wanted outside our family budget, we had to save for it— but a junior golf membership came with a higher price tag than anything on my wish list to date. Like most kids, I would have preferred the easier path of my parents springing for it, but looking back, it instilled strong financial habits to work hard and save for things I wanted.

Years later, between my junior and senior years in college, I was offered an internship with a financial advisor. I knew it wasn't the norm to score a paid internship, so I jumped at the opportunity. The income was nice, but even better was what my time there sparked: an interest in investing and the vision of a career helping others in the arena of financial planning.

Prior to the internship, I hadn't had the faintest idea what a financial advisor did. But after a few months at the firm, I knew it was what I wanted to do after college. I admit, it also didn't hurt that my boss was a member of a golf club. The idea of being able to help people with their money and eventually afford a golf club membership appealed to me as an ambitious guy in his early twenties.

With guidance from my advisor, I applied at a variety of companies, ultimately landing a position with Morgan Stanley. At the time, many financial advisory businesses were shifting to a fiduciary, fee-based model. In simple terms, *fiduciary* means acting in the best interest of a client. This encompasses understanding a client's financial objectives and circumstances, disclosing any conflicts of interest, and applying skill, diligence, and prudence in support of achieving clients' goals. By incentivizing employees to focus on fiduciary work, Morgan Stanley, for one, became more confident in planning long-term revenue strategies. This model was also favorable to commission-based selling, which is not always conducted in a client's best interest.

Within this framework, at the end of three years I received a bonus based on how much fiduciary-type work I had accomplished. Although employees were not prohibited from making commission-based sales, the emphasis on fiduciary work led to reduced focus on commissions because of the incentives the company provided not to engage in this way. Still, it soon became clear to me that working for a large firm was no longer for me.

These "stable" companies that were long viewed as "too big to fail" almost went out of business during the 2008 financial crisis. Not only that, it was later revealed that some were selling questionable products to people, such as short-term municipal bonds—known as municipal-backed securities (MBS)—that lost a ton of money. This led to lawsuits and settlements that caused great harm to clients. Though certainly not everyone at Morgan Stanley was guilty of this, I didn't want to be affiliated with a company that put its clients at risk, so I decided to establish an independent firm, one in which I would never be associated with practices that weren't completely aligned with my values.

Today, I am a proponent of working on a fee-only basis, which is the arrangement I recommend to anyone seeking to partner with a financial planner. In this type of partnership, there is no selling of questionable investments that could lead to questionable commissions and recommendations; instead, I either offer a flat fee engagement for financial planning only, or work on a percentage of the assets I oversee for investment management (which carries an investment minimum) and financial planning together, depending on the needs of the client. This allows me to make recommendations that are always based on what is best for the client, rather than which investment pays me the highest commission.

My decision to become an independent advisor and start my own practice centered on the fiduciary model of planning was not an easy one, but it was definitely the right one. Unhindered by corporate directives, I am able to prioritize the needs of my clients above all else, which is what everyone deserves from a professional who's advising them on their investments and financial plan.

My goal in this book is to give you all the guidance you need to forge and maintain a beneficial partnership with a fiduciary financial advisor—whether you are looking to hire an advisor for the first time, or to re-evaluate a current partnership or investment strategy. With twenty-two years of experience shepherding my clients through life changes and changing financial markets, I will walk you through:

+ Why to hire a financial advisor versus managing your assets alone

+ The specific advantages of working within the fiduciary model

+ The critical elements you should look for when interviewing financial advisors

+ What to expect once you're in the partnership

+ Planning for your future with regard to retirement, insurance, taxes, and your estate

+ Creating a portfolio that is aligned with your life plan

+ Investment strategies to avoid

+ How to evaluate your partnership and portfolio to ensure both are delivering value to you

Armed with knowledge and a clear path, my hope is that I can assuage any trepidation you may feel about entrusting your assets to a financial advisor, empower you with solid expectations and enough understanding—without overwhelm—of the primary recommendations to feel confident, and embolden you with assurance that you *can* retire with ease and provide for your loved ones, even within the rapidly changing financial landscape we are in today.

You can do this. And I am grateful to be in a position to help.

1

WHY HIRE A
FINANCIAL ADVISOR?

———◇———

E ven if you consider yourself to be good with money, and
possibly even have some investing experience under your
belt, there are several reasons to consider hiring a financial advisor:

+ You arrive at a significant life event, such as having a
  child, getting married, buying or selling a home,
  planning for college, retiring, getting divorced, losing a
  spouse, inheriting a large sum of money, or buying,
  starting, or selling a business

+ You'd like a professional to help you manage your
  investments so that you can maximize your returns for
  yourself or your family

+ You need guidance on the most beneficial decisions
  regarding retirement savings, insurance, taxes, and/or
  estate planning

No matter which of these may apply to you, a good financial advisor can be an indispensable ally in the growth of your assets. Not only do they keep their finger on the pulse of industry changes and sound strategies, but they know how to navigate the unique issues that significant life events carry, and it can be helpful to have someone who has helped clients manage these situations before so that you can avoid mistakes and take advantage of opportunities.

It's true that not all financial advisors have the same skill set, or run their businesses in the same way. In the next chapter, we'll discuss why I recommend the fiduciary model above all others, and in Chapter 3, we'll dive into the essentials to look for when seeking the right financial advisor for you. But for now, I want to give you a sense of why a financial advisor can be an ally, and why going it alone can often have consequences that aren't so favorable.

There is a school of thought that you don't need a financial advisor, that you can manage your assets yourself. But, as with any profession, a great deal of study and skill is required to do the job well, and this is certainly true of the financial industry. Most people don't have the time or the passion to delve into the nitty gritty of the financial landscape; I personally spend hundreds of hours a year reading about financial planning strategies, taxes, investing, and changes in legislation, merely to stay on the cutting edge. You may share a similar passion for finance—reading blogs and books, and listening to podcasts—and that's great; you may be one of the few who can manage a portfolio on your own. But if you're not going to invest that kind of time, or if you have no interest in doing so, you probably shouldn't be your own financial planner. Yes, there are plenty of websites out there that show you how to manage your assets, and you may get 20 to 30 percent of it done the right way. But missing the other 70 to 80 percent can significantly impact your long-term success. A long-term perspective and solid investment strategy not only improves your investment performance, but it also helps you capitalize on excellent opportunities.

One of the biggest mistakes people make in going solo is relying on the worst possible guidepost to investing: the main-stream media. In fact, financial TV channels such as Fox Business or CNBC are often referred to as "financial pornography" by financial advisors. This is because most of the individuals offering opinions on these outlets have no real accountability when it comes to the advice they dispense. Their prognostications are often based on little more than guesswork, and the guidance they give is inherently short term in nature. Consequently, the notion that one can gain a significant advantage in the markets by constantly monitoring the media is misguided. A great deal of money is poured into Wall Street every day to try to help people figure out what's going to occur in the markets, but most of that is merely noise.

The bottom line is: it's extremely challenging for the average person to invest the time in the correct resources to understand everything they need to know about portfolio management. It's much better to focus on your family, your career, and on increasing your income. While you're working, your financial advisor will be working *for* you, allowing you to focus on your priorities while they focus on the financial side of things. And you can sleep better at night knowing you have a long-term plan, not worrying about catching this or that news story for some possible short-term gain that may not even be viable.

WHEN SHOULD I ENGAGE A FINANCIAL ADVISOR?

As noted at the beginning of the chapter, there are several reasons to think about hiring a financial advisor. We'll review each one briefly here.

1. Having a Child

You not only want to ensure your income is being allotted for the expense of raising a child, but also for their future needs, such as education; extracurriculars, such as sports, music, dance, art, camps, and the like; religious or coming-of-age celebrations; health needs; and incidentals, such as travel opportunities, creative endeavors, etc. You also want to plan ahead in the unfortunate event that something happens to you and/or your spouse.

2. Getting Married

A wedding of any size will require some expenditure, and having a solid understanding of what you can comfortably afford is vital so that you don't enter wedded bliss with a pile of not-so-blissful debt.

3. Buying a Home / Selling a Home

There are a multitude of expenses when buying a home—down payment, escrow fees, realtor fees, improvement costs, mortgage payment, property taxes, possible HOA fees, and the like. You also want to feel secure that you can deal with the upkeep of your home as those expenses arise. Selling a home may also carry financial challenges for you, such that sound advice would be helpful to receive.

4. Planning for College

It goes without saying that the earlier you begin to put away for your child's education, the better. But no matter when you start, it's helpful to have a realistic sum you can invest for this purpose, knowing you will have the desired amount when your child reaches college age. It can also be helpful to know which colleges and universities may be most affordable for you and your child, along with the best ways to pay for college expenses.

5. Retiring

By the time you reach your mid to late fifties, you will likely be thinking about retirement. Whether you work for a company or run your own business, knowing what you need to retire comfortably and have the life you desire is crucial at this point. Starting earlier is preferable, but most people get serious about retirement planning in their midfifties, when the reality of retirement starts to hit them. Even if you hire an advisor on a one-time basis for a limited engagement, they can help you ensure you're on track for your retirement goals. (We will discuss retirement planning in greater detail in Chapter 5.)

6. Getting Divorced

The emotional stress of a divorce is difficult enough; having help with the financial side can be a lifesaver. Whether you are the giver or receiver of alimony, there are children to support, or there is a home to consider selling or splitting, sound financial guidance during a divorce can offer abundant peace of mind.

7. Losing a Spouse

The devastation of losing a spouse can be life-shattering, no matter the circumstance or age. When this occurs, a financial advisor can help guide on wills and trusts, pension and Social Security, funeral expenses, and other concerns, such as when the surviving spouse must suddenly live on a single income, willed assets must be divided, and the like.

8. Inheriting a Large Sum of Money

An inheritance can be a huge gift that in the immediate solves some financial burdens. But to keep your inheritance from slowly (or quickly) diminishing, it's wise to have financial guidance so that the money can continue to grow for you.

9. Buying, Starting, or Selling a Business

Whether you're buying, starting, or selling a business, the substantial asset of an entire business has multiple facets, no matter how large or small. A financial advisor can go over all of these with you to ensure all your bases are covered in receiving/paying what's appropriate, planning for further costs, and going forward with your profits.

10. Help with Receiving the Best Returns on the Earnings You Invest / General Money Management

As we've already discussed, it takes a great deal of time and understanding of the industry to study financial markets on your own. Engaging a financial advisor who knows the most appropriate investments for your life circumstance, as well as general management of the money you earn, can provide significant peace of mind, as well as valuable returns.

11. Guidance on Necessities

While most people think of a financial advisor for retirement, many don't know that they can also advise on other necessities, such as insurance, taxes, and estate planning. While these typically require other professionals too—agents, accountants, and attorneys—a financial advisor can look at the entire picture of your financial health and give you sound guidance on what you need, as opposed to each of these elements only being considered individually.

WHAT IF I ALREADY HAVE A PORTFOLIO?

If you've tried unsuccessfully to manage your own portfolio, you have a portfolio with another advisor but are seeking to hire a new one because yours isn't a good match for you, or you simply want to invest better than you currently are, you may want to hire a financial advisor to evaluate your asset allocation and identify areas for improvement.

When meeting with prospective clients, I examine how they've invested their money and/or assess what their current financial advisor has been doing. If I see unfavorable products, poor investment strategies, or a lack of management from their current advisor, I will inform them without sugarcoating. For example, I often find that clients hold high-cost mutual fund products or annuities. When this is the case, my firm helps them reallocate their monies to a more suitable lower-cost index-based portfolio. Once we establish the new strategy, I ensure the client is aware of both the best- and worst-case scenarios so that they know what to expect and can stay the course over the long term.

With all of these factors laid out, I hope you can see the clear advantages of having a financial advisor on your team, particularly within the fiduciary model this book is based on. Which leads us into our next chapter: Transparency, Trust, Triumph: Why the Fiduciary Model Is Best for You as a Client and an Investor.

2

TRANSPARENCY, TRUST, TRIUMPH

Why the Fiduciary Model Is Best for You as a Client and an Investor

——◦——

I am a staunch proponent of the fiduciary model for multiple reasons, but mainly because at its core, it represents the essence of ethical behavior: that financial advisors have an obligation to act in their clients' best interests above their own at all times. This obligation functions on three foundational premises: 1) that the advisor is **transparent** with clients; 2) that transparency honestly earns the **trust** of their client; and 3) that the advisor delivers on guiding clients to **triumph**, not to tragedy, with their financial well-being.

This may sound overly simplistic, and possibly even obvious. Why would anyone hire and keep a financial advisor who wasn't transparent, they didn't trust, or didn't cause them to triumph financially? Unfortunately, this *does* happen more than I wish it did: people who don't know what questions to ask, what strategies to avoid, or how to evaluate performance—all things I will teach you in this book—will often find themselves in a less-than-favorable partnership with a financial advisor. This typically occurs because they aren't working with an authentic fiduciary, meaning an advisor who takes ethics seriously and who runs their business on a fee-only basis.

A fiduciary typically operates on a percentage of a client's portfolio, wherein they provide advice and management services—and that is the only fee they ever charge. In my firm, for example, our fee structure starts at 1.25 percent and can decrease to 1 percent or even lower, depending on the total amount of assets we manage for the client. (Typically, advisors adjust their fee down for larger portfolios.) To get an understanding of how this model can benefit you:

> Say you have a $200,000 portfolio, and we charge you 1.25 percent annually to manage it, which is $2,500. As a result of our advice and management, your portfolio grows to $300,000. At this level, our fee percentage remains the same: 1.25 percent, or $3,750. Yes, the increase in portfolio size translates to more revenue for us, but your portfolio has grown as well. In other words, our incentive is still aligned with your best interest, as we are motivated to help you grow your portfolio. At the same time, if your portfolio decreases to $150,000 because we've given you bad advice, you've withdrawn money, or the market has experienced a downturn, we get paid less: $1,875. In short, we are in a win-win or lose-lose structure, never a lose-win, whereby you as a client lose but we as advisors win. Within this mutually

beneficial relationship, when our clients do better financially, we also do better.

You may initially balk at paying a set fee, but understand that the percentage you pay is worth much more than what it may look like on the surface. (We will compare the fiduciary fee with commission-based fees and kickbacks shortly.) The value of fiduciary services includes portfolio management, counseling, and ongoing planning, which can encompass retirement, insurance, taxes, and estate, cash flow management, college planning, and much more. It also includes coordinating with other professionals such as accountants, attorneys, bankers, and insurance agents to ensure you're getting the best advice possible and receiving the most value for what you're paying. Different firms have varied specialties, but overall, when you're looking at the fee a fiduciary charges, those are the types of services you can expect.

With regard to fees, I recommend you look for the following:

+ Availability of the fee schedule on the advisor's website, so that potential clients can determine what charges to expect

+ The signing of an agreement, after hiring your advisor, indicating you understand and agree with the fee structure

+ Delivery of a quarterly statement that shows what you paid the firm, ensuring complete transparency in their transactions

While the percentage-of-assets fee is the most common within the fiduciary model, note that clients may also work with their advisors on a flat fee or one-time fee basis, as well as on an hourly basis, though the latter is the most rare of the fee arrangement options.

Another aspect with regard to fees is that research has consistently shown lower fees have a high correlation to long-term investor success. For example, a 2016 study by MorningStar titled "Predictive Power of Fees" found that investments with lower costs were many times more likely to earn a successful return when compared to those that were more expensive. In short, where you can minimize your investment fees, you are going to add to your bottom line.

Last, you should always feel the services you're receiving are in alignment with the fee you're paying (more on this in Chapter 8.) In my firm, for example, if a client expresses that our services aren't worth what they're paying, I advise them to discontinue the partnership. Though this is a rare occurrence, it is nonetheless in line with our ethics. You, as a client, must receive value for what you pay for, and if you don't believe this is the case with your advisor, you have every right to leave and seek another.

BEING AWARE OF PRODUCT SALESPEOPLE MASQUERADING AS FINANCIAL ADVISORS

Fee-only financial advisors, who are held to a higher standard, should always serve as ethical examples in the industry and base their business on transparency and accessibility. However, as in any business, there are imposters who don't live up to their fiduciary duty. In the next chapter, we will dive into interviewing financial advisors to ensure you're partnering with a true fiduciary who operates with your best interest at heart, but for now, I want to explain the difference between working with an ethical fiduciary and with an advisor who works on commission and kickbacks.

I may sound like a record that plays only one song, but if you're looking to achieve what I call "financial nirvana," the best way to get there is to work with a fee-only financial planner.

Within this arrangement:

+ The advisor can develop a well-balanced portfolio for you with reasonable costs, utilizing an index-based strategy.

+ The advisor can help you examine your overall financial plan and take you through a process to address all areas of financial planning through a series of meetings.

+ You will know exactly what you're paying for, thanks to transparency.

+ Your advisor will be responsive and will coordinate with other professionals when necessary.

+ You will receive solid value for what you're paying.

While there *are* good advisors who are not fiduciaries and provide this level of service to their clients, I have found that the majority of satisfied clients work within the fiduciary model. Outside of that model, such as with brokers or with those who call themselves financial advisors or planners but work within a whole different framework, is when I've seen people enter what I call the realm of "financial hell."

This occurs when clients partner with individuals who aren't actually financial advisors, but rather salespeople who only contact you when they want to sell you high-fee products. These brokers and insurance salespeople refer to themselves as financial advisors, but they're primarily focused on selling products, not on providing comprehensive financial advice. In truth, these individuals are not equipped to offer personalized financial guidance, and their clients may not even realize they're receiving inadequate support until it's too late. Sometimes clients place trust in this person because they are a friend, family member, or were referred to them, and therefore ignore the detrimental guidance, more concerned with offending their advisor than firing them.

Unfortunately, within this type of arrangement, you will almost always:

+ have poor investment results
+ receive little to no financial planning support
+ pay more taxes than you should on your investment portfolio
+ have no scheduled review meetings
+ not be aware of what other options are available to you

Even if there are specific products or services you need that your financial advisor can't provide through their network, I still would not advise you to work directly with one of these product pushers. Best is for your financial advisor to work in conjunction with salespeople to obtain products outside their network on your behalf. This way, you are working with your fiduciary advisor, who has your best interest at heart.

THE DETRIMENT OF COMMISSIONS AND KICKBACKS

Although some advisors in the brokerage world strive to do the right things for their clients, there are simply too many who are motivated by a singular incentive: earning commission and/or kickbacks on what they sell. Within this model lies a fundamental misalignment of interests between advisors and clients. To put it bluntly, this misalignment can cause advisors to recommend products that are in *their* best interest, not in the clients'. Some products may be outright inappropriate for the client yet they offer high commissions or incentives—and because clients may not fully understand how these "advisors" get paid, they are unaware of the blatant conflict of interest.

The analogy I give prospective clients is that working with product peddlers disguised as advisors is like being asleep during a house fire—everything's ablaze around you, but you can't smell the smoke. These salespeople using the advisor title and who are incentivized by commissions often feel compelled to sell a product to get paid. After all, an advisor doesn't typically want to spend four or five hours with a client for free; they have to receive compensation in some way—and that is through selling you something. That "something" may be an unsafe or reckless investment, insurance you don't need, etc., simply because the incentive is high for the advisor. Over time, you will likely come to realize that you've lost money you could have invested more profitably, or wasted payments on premiums for unnecessary insurance, to name only two.

In the worst-case scenario, financial advisors—either masquerading as fiduciaries or failing to work as such—steal from their clients. Fortunately, this doesn't happen often, but if you've ever seen the show *American Greed*, you know these unconscionable acts occur—advisors who steer clients toward bad recommendations, put them in garbage investment products, and charge fees way above the norm, all to earn commissions. It's despicable. If the client or their family uncovers the fraud and sues the advisor, the advisor could—and should—lose their securities or insurance license, forfeit the financial credentials they may have, and be barred from the industry.

Alongside commissions, advisors (again, more in name only) often also receive compensation in the form of kickbacks, such as monetary bonuses, trips, fancy dinners, and the like. While it's possible that individual advisors are unaware that their firm is receiving kickbacks, this practice is not uncommon, and some independent advisors fall prey to the kickback lure as well.

For one example, during the time I worked for a large firm, I attended annual conferences where investment companies were present. They would host mini classes to educate us on what was going on within the industry and how to better help our clients. While there was nothing wrong with that, these events were also an opportunity for investment companies to promote their products, often with kickbacks. The ethical concern didn't end there, though. These companies also often subsidized part of the conference cost, and hawking their products was a way to recoup that investment. In short, it created an ugly cycle that was a clear conflict of interest.

The bottom line is: If these large firms were product-agnostic, receiving no kickbacks from investment companies, they would be better positioned to provide beneficial outcomes for their *clients*, rather than for themselves. While advisors who work for these large firms are typically free to choose the products they recommend to clients, they may feel pressure to maintain relationships with investment companies that offer perks, ultimately influencing their recommendations. In contrast, by focusing solely on helping clients choose the best products and investments for their particular life circumstances, *without incentives or kickbacks being a factor*, clients are more likely to invest in products that meet their needs and at lower costs.

As an investor, knowing how financial advisors are compensated can help you avoid receiving bad advice or investing in deleterious products. This is, again, why I will always recommend working with a fiduciary aligned with the values of that title. When you do, worries of back-end compensation and honest motivation are not a factor; you pay your percentage or flat fee, and your fiduciary only prospers when you do.

In full disclosure, I have reviewed prospective clients' statements and observed instances of poor advice given under the fiduciary model too. But, in my experience, this tends to occur with larger, nationally recognized firms. These firms charge a percentage of a client's assets, also known as an AUM, or "assets under management" fee, for managing their money. While this doesn't differ from the fiduciary model, what *does* differ is that many of these firms also receive kickbacks from mutual fund companies. This is due to a practice referred to as "shelf space," where mutual fund companies offer commissions to carry their funds on the firm's platforms. There is a cost to the firm to carry these funds, which is passed on to the client in the form of higher mutual fund fees. Hence, companies that are willing to pay more for shelf space may get more exposure and are therefore sold more frequently, even if their products are not the best fit for clients. These firms may also charge their clients additional fees to recoup their costs, which perpetuates the cycle of prioritizing profits over clients.

And it doesn't end there. In some cases, mutual fund companies who don't offer shelf space commissions are manipulated by firms into paying fees. I once witnessed this firsthand while attending a conference, where I overheard a national sales manager on the phone with an investment company say that if they wanted to do business with his firm, they needed to pay to be given access to the platform or they wouldn't be considered. They might have had an excellent product for the advisors' clients, but they had to pay for shelf space to be able to offer it.

Again, these unscrupulous practices perpetuate a cycle that not only hurts clients but the financial advisory industry as well, as the best mutual funds with the lowest fees are often kept off their platforms because they refuse to "pay to play." Fortunately, this is not the norm with fee-only advisors.

Now that we've talked about avoiding "financial hell," let's return to the fiduciary model and recap the reasons it is advantageous for you as an investor. Though I cannot make the claim that every fiduciary will fulfill each of these tenets and commitments, as a general rule, the value system of a fiduciary supports the following.

1. A fiduciary is a fee-only financial advisor/planner, meaning they are not licensed to sell any products that would pay them a commission, such as insurance or investment products, or receive kickbacks, as in vacations

or monetary perks. Instead, clients pay them a predetermined fee for their services, and that is all they pay.

2. A fiduciary is obligated to help you do what's best with your money, rather than merely sell you a product. This puts you as a client in a better position to make informed investment decisions from the start.

3. The fiduciary model minimizes conflicts of interest, since advisors are not incentivized to recommend certain products. Therefore, clients seeking advice are unlikely to encounter any significant conflicts of interest. If any potential conflicts to the client are present before forging a partnership, a fiduciary is bound to disclose that.

4. Fiduciaries are much more likely to give clients an honest assessment of their situation when it comes to what assets they have and what they may want to invest in or achieve in terms of savings and planning. This honest feedback is essential, as clients sometimes have unrealistic expectations about their financial situation.

5. Fiduciaries are committed to staying on the cutting edge of what will best help their clients maximize their return and minimize their fees, within the risk they're comfortable taking in their portfolios.

6. Fiduciaries will schedule joint meetings with other professionals, making sure their clients are receiving the best advice in areas not within their specific expertise. They will endeavor to build a team for their clients, or if the client comes to the partnership with an existing

team, ensure that the team is functioning and communicating well.

7. Fiduciaries are committed to being lifelong learners, constantly striving to stay up to date with the latest industry trends, advancements, and laws. While they may believe their current processes are effective, they remain open to the possibility of discovering better processes or products that could benefit their clients, as well as staying abreast of legislative changes that affect investment strategies.

8. Fiduciaries continue to work with their clients through various life situations, not merely send them on their way after one meeting and hope for the best. They stay involved and offer support where it's needed.

9. Fiduciaries hold no other licenses, such as an insurance or brokerage license, which again negates any conflicts of interest.

10. Fiduciaries assist clients with insurance, tax, or estate planning questions with the same fee arrangement that is already in place, and they receive no incentives for referrals to other professionals.

11. Although there is no guarantee, a fiduciary arrangement puts you in the best position for your capital to be utilized in the most efficient manner, allowing more of it to remain in your pocket rather than be needlessly spent on costs and fees that benefit others.

12. Fiduciaries achieve personal fulfillment by putting their clients' needs ahead of their own, by working collaboratively to achieve their clients' financial objectives, and by providing honest, unbiased advice that establishes their reputation as a trusted and reliable advisor.

13. On a percentage-based fee, when a fiduciary helps you make more money, they earn more money. If they don't do well for you and your assets decrease, they will earn less. With these interests aligned, it allows your advisor to provide you with the best possible service and advice.

In sum, I sincerely believe that achieving industry nirvana entails all advisors working within the fiduciary model, fully aligned with its principles as the standard. But until that happens, I hope this chapter inspires you to seek a "nirvana" experience with the advisor you hire. If this turns out not to be the case, look for someone else to manage your finances who is a good match for your personality, your goals, and your expectations. Your money is too important to leave in the hands of someone who is not delivering for you. Excellent fiduciaries are everywhere. Once you find the right one, it is my fervent hope that you'll maintain a long and prosperous relationship.

In the next chapter, I'll walk you through the process of finding an authentic fiduciary, what red flags to be aware of, and how to be best aligned with an advisor who can meet your needs for your specific life circumstances and goals.

3

FINDING YOUR IDEAL MATCH

The Essentials to Look For in a Financial Advisor

———•———

As you embark on considering financial advisors, I understand the overwhelm and trepidation you may feel. You undoubtedly want to know: What should I look for? What should I ask? What's the norm and what's a potential red flag? How do I avoid getting taken by a charlatan? In this chapter, I'll take you through these essentials in an easy-to digest way, not only to empower you and instill confidence, but to give you peace of mind that you have all the information you need to discern the ideal advisor for you.

Let's begin by getting clear on titles. One of the biggest sources of confusion for clients when looking for the right financial advisor lies in the titles that people in the financial world claim. Unfortunately, there is not always a clear distinction between product salespeople—such as investment brokers, insurance brokers, or stockbrokers—and true financial advisors. Part of this problem is that there isn't a hard and fast standard; if brokers want to call themselves "financial advisors," they're not prohibited from doing so. However, more often than not, they're not *advising* but rather *selling*. Also, they are not registered investment advisors. The differences between the two are manyfold, as laid out in the chart below.

Brokers	Registered Investment Advisors
They are salespeople (investment products, insurance)	They are fiduciaries
They can call themselves financial advisors, though they are not held to a fiduciary standard	They are held to the Investment Advisors Act of 1940
They have no requirement to put the client's interest ahead of their own	They are required to put the client's interest ahead of their own
They are not required to disclose conflicts of interest or commissions they make	They are required to disclose any conflicts of interest and their fees
Their obligation is to their brokerage firm	Their obligation is to their clients
They are compensated for more sales and turnover	They are compensated on an hourly basis, fixed-fee, or percentage of the assets they advise on
They receive commission and kickbacks from the products and investments they recommend	They receive no commission or kickbacks from the products and investments they recommend
Any advice they give is incidental	Any advice they give is in the best interest of the client

While I don't want to paint the picture that all brokers are only out for themselves, or that no one should ever work with a specialized broker for a specific reason, in terms of hiring someone to advise you on your financial health, you can see the stark differences between brokers and registered financial advisors. Even though I started out as a broker, and I used to give brokers the benefit of the doubt, the longer I work in this field, the more I see poorly constructed investment portfolios provided by brokers, with high-fee products and low returns. Some of these products may even include additional fees paid to the advisor that the client is unaware of. So, if you want to get the most out of your money, I firmly believe that avoiding brokers and engaging in fee-only financial planning is how you will be best served as a client.

As we've already discussed in Chapter 2, in a perfect world, anyone using the title "financial advisor" or "financial planner" would adhere to fiduciary standards. Yet because this isn't the case—at least not yet—let me offer you a brief summation of these general titles and what they customarily mean.

A *financial advisor* typically advises on investments and helps manage your investment portfolio. Some also offer financial planning, such as for retirement, insurance, taxes, and your estate. Note that this can vary, as not all advisors will specialize in every aspect of one's finances, but rather on a select few.

A *financial planner* does not typically advise on or manage any investments; instead, the focus is centered on improving money management, as well as on saving for retirement.

While there is a distinction between an advisor and planner most of the time, the terms "financial advisor" and "financial planner" are often used interchangeably. For both titles, however, the Certified Financial Planning designation (CFP®) is a highly regarded credential.

And as a brief recap:

A *broker* is someone who sells financial products yet may call himself a financial advisor *or* a financial planner. His primary job is selling products and earning commissions and kickbacks on those products, but he may "advise" on which products are good for a client. As we've already discussed, this advice may not be in the client's best interest, but he still calls himself a "financial advisor."

This leads us back to the first and most critical underlying quality in an advisor we discussed in the previous chapter: **transparency**. When a financial advisor is committed to transparency, the **trust** and the **triumph** naturally follow. You will know precisely what their title encompasses, how they operate, and what ethical standards they adhere to.

Are all fiduciaries completely transparent? Though I wish I could say yes, as in any business, there are a few unscrupulous ones who aren't. I have also found people who are insurance brokers calling themselves fiduciaries. Unfortunately there is no regulatory body enforcing the use of the term *fiduciary*; you as the client must dig deeper to verify that the title is authentic (I will guide you on this shortly). But after twenty-two years in this industry, I can say that in my experience, the majority of clients who work with authentic fiduciaries have the longest relationships and the most gratifying outcomes.

DETERMINING YOUR NEEDS

Now that you have some clarity around the distinctions in titles, it's important you know what your needs are in hiring a financial advisor. Here is a list of common needs you can assess. Write down or mark all that apply to you.

+ general money management
+ investment strategies
+ ongoing investment management
+ planning and/or investing for a new child / current children
+ planning and/or investing for a wedding and new life as a couple
+ dealing with financial situations surrounding a divorce
+ buying or selling a home
+ planning for college
+ planning for retirement
+ dealing with financial situations surrounding the loss of a spouse
+ inheritance of a large sum of money
+ buying, starting, or selling a business
+ analyzing tax returns and collaborating with your accountant
+ guidance on insurance

- guidance on taxation, in general
- guidance on estate planning
- guidance on wills and trusts
- guidance on stock options

CONDUCTING RUDIMENTARY RESEARCH

With a solid list of what your needs are, and therefore the type of advisory skills and specialties you may be seeking, it's time to conduct some research on the financial advisors you're considering hiring. (Note that I prefer to use the term "financial advisor" and will going forward, though a "financial planner" may provide you with certain similar services.)

The advisors you research may come from referrals, or from a web search. Here are the search terms and sites I recommend to find advisors in your area or your state (meeting in person is no longer a requirement now that we have video conferencing, so your advisor does not have to be local).

- You can do a search for "fee-only advisors in [city, state]"
- You can visit the following websites and search for advisors near you:
  - ✓ www.XYPlanningNetwork.com
  - ✓ www.feeonlynetwork.com
  - ✓ www.NAPFA.org (fee-only advisors)
  - ✓ www.thefiduciarystandard.org
  - ✓ www.CFP.net (CFP stands for Certified Financial Planners). Note that this site includes non-

fiduciaries, so you will need to weed out anyone who is listed as a broker.

Whether you find your fee-only advisor via referral, web search, or one of the sites above, I highly recommend you do a bit of investigating of the following before calling to set up a meeting.

The Advisor's / Firm's Website

+ Do they state that they are a fee-only advisor? (Most who are will plainly state this.)

+ Do they have at least one certification after their name, such as the CFP® designation? (I will highlight others in the Top Ten Questions section to follow)

+ Do they state their specializations?

+ Do the firm's advisors have credible experience in their bios?

If all of these are represented clearly on their website, that's a step in the right direction. If you have any sense that transparency is lacking—the fees aren't listed or aren't easily found, how they conduct business isn't clear, they don't have any certifications, etc.—I recommend moving on to another advisor's site.

The BrokerCheck Website

+ Navigate to **https://brokercheck.finra.org**, a site maintained by FINRA, the Financial Industry Regulatory Authority.

✦ Search for the advisor's name and verify that they are registered under the Investment Advisor Act of 1940. This is important because in 1999, Merrill Lynch won a lawsuit against the SEC that allowed them to be exempt from the Investment Advisor Act of 1940, even though they were offering advice and collecting an advisory fee for this advice. In other words, they were acting as *financial advisors*, even though they were actually registered as *brokers*. This is known as the Merrill Lynch Rule. Since that case, there has been confusion because "financial advisor" used to mean a fiduciary, and only fee-only financial advisors could use that term. If this distinction were still in place, it would be easier for consumers to know who they were dealing with, but until that changes, I recommend verifying an advisor's registration under the 1940 Act.

Note: If they are listed here as a broker, they are not a fee-only advisor and I recommend crossing them off your list.

✦ Access the BrokerCheck report that shows the advisor's licenses, work history, and any complaints filed against them.

Here I want to make clear why complaints are filed, why they may not be concerning, and why they may be a red flag.

If a client has a complaint against their advisor, and that advisor is registered as a broker, their broker-dealer (aka parent company) has an obligation to report that complaint and further investigate it. (As you know, I don't advocate for partnerships with brokers; however, I'm mentioning it here because it may apply if your chosen advisor was previously registered as a broker.) Generally, the complaint is forwarded to the compliance department at their broker-dealer. Some advisors could try to hide that complaint, but that could be grounds for termination if they are found out. If a client has a complaint against their advisor (who is not a broker), it is typically submitted in writing to their supervisor or compliance department. In either case, only damages over $5,000 are reported.

Typically, clients agree to arbitration when they open an investment account. The arbitration procedure allows each side to present facts, and then the arbitrator makes the decision. If the arbitrator finds in favor of the client, and the client receives compensation, it would then be reported on the client's Form U4 and on Broker-Check. In that report, you'll see something akin to, "Client filed the complaint for $10,000. Found in favor of the client. Awarded X." Or it could say, "Client filed the complaint, but it was not found in favor of the client. No damages awarded."

A complaint being filed does not necessarily indicate a problem, but multiple complaints and awards could be indicative of issues with an advisor.

As a side note to you as an investor: In my experience, while there's no statistical information to support this, a lot of complaints are associated with annuities. In my professional opinion, many types of annuities are not suitable for clients due to their high fees and potential lock-up periods (more on annuities in Chapter 6). However, it's important for financial advisors to disclose these details to clients and ensure they understand the product before making a decision. Unfortunately, there have been multiple cases where clients were not fully informed, and as a result, they have wanted their money back.

In sum, do look up any complaints that may exist for the advisor you're considering. Those above $5,000, even if found to be baseless, are disclosed in this report. As I've said, complaints may not justify a problem with an advisor, but they do often call ethics and an advisor's ability to communicate into question. Yes, some complaints are indeed baseless and unfortunately leave a mark on the advisor's record, but if you discover multiple complaints against an advisor, it's best to steer clear.

The SEC Website

+ Once you've confirmed through BrokerCheck that your financial advisor is not a broker, navigate to **https://adviserinfo.sec.gov**—or simply click on the link to the SEC website—to look up the advisor's name and reference the two documents you can obtain from the SEC.

  ✓ The first is the advisor's **IAPD report**. It is similar to the report available on BrokerCheck in that it contains information on the advisor's employment history, professional qualification, disciplinary actions, criminal convictions, and arbitration awards. Here you can verify the services the advisor provides and any conflicts of interest they may have, such as whether they hold an insurance or stockbroker license.

✓ The second is called an **ADV**, a disclosure document required by the SEC for every registered investment advisory firm. There are two parts to an ADV: Part 1 contains the official information required each year by the SEC; and Part 2 is a summary of that information. I suggest you review both, but if you want a quick summary, you can review Part 2 only.

Note that if you have trouble finding the firm's ADV, you can access what's called the CRD number to look up their firm. You can also search by their firm name, but be aware that if there are multiple firms with similar names, it can be tricky to find them. To make it easier on clients, many firms have a link to their ADV 2 on their website, as my firm does. **Note also that before you do business with a registered investment advisor, they are required to send you a copy of their ADV 2.**

✦ If both the IAPD report and the ADV come back clean, and you see no conflicts of interest, I recommend moving forward with scheduling a meeting, where you will want to ask the advisor the questions that follow.

THE TOP TEN INTERVIEW QUESTIONS TO ASK A FINANCIAL ADVISOR

Early in my independent practice, I formulated ten questions that I recommend all clients ask a prospective financial advisor to ensure you're matched with the right one for your particular needs. These questions (and the answers my firm provides) are available on my website at:

http://tinyurl.com/10questionsforadvisors

We'll go through each question here, with the answers I recommend you seek for the most beneficial outcome.

1. Are you a fiduciary and a fee-only firm? Will you sign the fiduciary pledge?

Obviously, the answer you want to hear to both questions is yes. The first part should be clear from the advisor's website, but I still recommend you ask directly. Again, this is to ensure there are no conflicts of interest. As an illustration to drive home why: Imagine going to see a doctor about a hip problem, and without the doctor examining you or performing any diagnostic tests, he sells you on getting a hip replacement. Further, the doctor says you need to act today before prices go up. You agree and after the surgery, you find out not only that the doctor was paid a bonus and received a free Hawaiian vacation for selling you the hip replacement, but that it cost more than it should have. While absurd for the medical profession, these practices unfortunately go on every day with non-fiduciary advisors.

The second part of the question references the Fiduciary Pledge. While not an official part of conferring credentials to a fiduciary, it is nonetheless a pledge that many fiduciaries voluntarily make. It states:

As defined by the committee for the fiduciary standard, I pledge to uphold the five responsibilities fiduciaries are committed to:

- √ **to put a client's interest first;**
- √ **to act with utmost good faith;**
- √ **to provide full and adequate disclosure of all material facts;**
- √ **not to mislead clients; and**
- √ **to expose all conflicts of interest to clients.**

If you'd like to download a copy for your fiduciary to sign, you can do so on my website at: https://www.morrisseywealthmanagement.com/free-resources.

2. Do you have any disclosures or complaints?

You have already looked up this information on the Broker-Check website and the SEC website, so this question is meant to ensure the advisor is truthful. If he or she claims to have no complaints, yet you have evidence of complaints from the Bro-kerCheck or the SEC site, you know you aren't interviewing a transparent and trustworthy person. And if you are interviewing someone who does have a few complaints but you've decided to consider them anyway, I advise asking why they were filed and how they responded to them. If anything feels off in the answers you're given, end the interview here and move on to the next advisor you're considering. It's not worth wasting your and the advisor's time, and it's definitely not worth having potential regrets in the future.

3. Do you have any specific certifications?

Again, any advisor who has completed the extensive study and testing to obtain certifications is going to display those after their name, and on their website. But to give you an understanding as a client of how credentials work, you should know that to become a fee-only fiduciary advisor, one only needs to attain what is called a Series 65 Securities License. It takes most people less than a few months of study to pass this exam, after which they are legally able to advise someone on their life savings. Pretty scary, right? Because of this limited training, most advisors seek additional education through varied financial designations. These credentials, or letters, after one's name, are sometimes referred to as "alphabet soup" because there are now so many of them.

Most experts agree that the most comprehensive and thorough is the Certified Financial Planning designation (CFP®). It takes most people a few years of study before they're prepared to sit for the CFP exam, which has only a 60 percent pass rate. An advisor is also required to have at least three years of financial planning experience to display the CFP mark. Only 20 percent of American financial advisors maintain the CFP designation, so it is a valuable distinction to look for. Other notable designations are CLU® (Chartered Life Underwriter), ChFC® (Chartered Financial Consultant), and CMFC® (Chartered Mutual Fund Consultant). All of these require many hours of study as well as thirty hours of ongoing education every two years to maintain them.

4. Do you have any specialties and what services do you offer?

As we discussed earlier, you want to be clear on what needs you have so that you can determine if the advisor will meet those particular needs. However, if you are unsure in any area, a competent, credentialed fiduciary will be able to guide you to the most appropriate services he or she offers, to achieve your specific goals.

Most fiduciaries specialize in some form of financial planning and wealth management. In my firm, for example, our two primary offerings are:

+ Comprehensive Financial Planning, which we refer to as the Retirement Readiness Report, for people interested in developing a comprehensive retirement plan. Comprehensive means the plan examines all areas of their financial lives: retirement planning, taxes, insurance, estate planning, and investments. This is performed for a flat fee and on a year-by-year basis.

+ Ongoing Wealth Management for clients interested in Comprehensive Financial Planning and Investment Management. This service combines both for one annual fee, based on the amount of assets we are managing for the client.

Here, you want to be aware of a potential red flag: If the advisor says they hold an insurance or stock broker license. You should have already been aware of this when you checked them on the SEC website, but just to reiterate, this means the advisor is a broker, and as you now know, a broker is in the business of selling products, and will therefore receive commissions. **Once again, you do not want to hire an advisor with any ties to commission-based earnings.** You want to stick with a fee-only fiduciary who doesn't have the conflicts of interest with stated "specialties," such as selling insurance or investment products. While they may act as a fiduciary on one side of your relationship, they act as a broker on the other, and you'll never know which hat they are wearing at any given time in your partnership. This is often the case when someone is a **fee-based** advisor, which means they are registered *both* as a broker and a registered investment advisor. Once again, I recommend steering clear of these people.

Another specialty is age-related. At my firm, our specialty is working with people 50 and older to help them plan for their retirement. To be fully educated in this arena, I have dedicated a significant amount of time to learning about Social Security, Medicare, retirement plans, retirement income, taxes, and estate planning. Other advisors may not possess adequate knowledge of these subjects, so if you are approaching the eligibility phase for Social Security and Medicare, or are focused on retirement, it would be prudent to seek the services of an advisor who is well versed in these areas. Otherwise, you may not receive optimal advice regarding these topics.

By the same token, perhaps you're looking for an advisor who works only with newly married couples or in a certain niche industry. Some advisors work solely within a certain field (such as eye doctors, for one example), or with executives who work for a specific company (such as Apple or Google). If this is your case, you will want to find an advisor who serves your niche with appropriate education and experience.

One more point: It *is* challenging, and quite rare, for a single financial advisor to be an expert at everything, which is why advisors typically focus on specific specialties. If, for example, your advisor's expertise is investment-focused, and not so much financial-planning focused, they should be transparent about that. If this comes up in your interview, ask if they have colleagues they recommend or would be willing to bring in an expert on your retirement plan so that you can decide what's best for you. You're trusting this person to guide you honestly, and you don't want it to be years before you realize you weren't receiving the most sage advice, and that you missed out on valuable planning opportunities that could have have delivered more profitable results.

5. How are you compensated for your services?

As we've already discussed, there are three ways fiduciaries are compensated: via a one-time flat fee, a percentage of managed assets, and an hourly rate (least common). Based on your needs, you should be offered one of these options. As examples for reference:

+ In my firm, for clients who engage us for Comprehensive Financial Planning, we are paid a flat fee (determined in advance of hiring). This fee generally begins at $4,000 per engagement. We collect half the fee once hired and the second half once the plan and recommendations have been delivered. We receive no additional fees or commissions from these clients.

✦ For clients who engage us for Ongoing Wealth Management, our fee is based on the assets under our management schedule, which is listed on our website. Clients receive a quarterly invoice detailing this fee, and it is also reflected in the statements provided by the custodian.

If the advisor has honestly answered yes to question number one—Are you a fiduciary and a fee-only firm?—then compensation red flags shouldn't be a factor. But remember, if the advisor mentions anything about receiving commissions or kickbacks when you ask this question, or you find it disclosed in their ADV, you know you're not working with a true fiduciary.

To be certain, don't leave it up to the advisor to disclose any conflicts of interest; ask directly if they receive these types of compensation at any time. If you want to be specific in your questioning, ask if they receive commissions on annuities, stocks or bonds, insurance of any kind, mutual funds, or limited partnerships in the form of a real estate trust. Ideally, an advisor who holds licenses to sell products of any kind will let those licenses go in favor of being a fee-only advisor, where they can eliminate these conflicts of interest.

In complete transparency, I want to add a note here on what may be considered a "conflict of interest," even with a fee-only advisor, and that is that you might be paying more to your advisor than if you managed your portfolio on your own. In other words, if you're someone who is a savvy investor, perhaps the total you pay to oversee your own portfolio is lower than the fee you would pay an advisor to do the same. A conflict may also be seen if your advisor recommends managing more of your portfolio, which means the advisor will be paid more. As we've discussed, this recommendation should always be made in your best interest, but it's something you should be aware of just the same.

6. What other costs will I be charged for?

A fiduciary advisor should always strive to keep your investment cost to a minimum, as this has a significant impact on your returns. As such, any additional fees should be minimal. In my firm, for example, clients who engage us for Ongoing Wealth Management generally have annual costs (fund expense ratios) for the funds we invest in their portfolio. In our case, portfolios mainly consist of Exchange Traded Funds (ETFs), and our average portfolio costs .09 percent per year, which, for reference, is below the current industry average of 1 percent.

Additional fees may apply from the custodians an advisor uses, such as trading costs and other charges, and those custodians must provide a fee schedule to all clients on an annual basis, which of course must then be disclosed to you. Do be aware that if you're told you'll be charged 1.5 to 2 percent commission on buying or selling a stock or bond, that's typically what "old school" brokers charge, which is much too high. Due to competition today, your fiduciary will likely use a discount broker for much less. I, for example, use Charles Schwab for mine and my clients' money, and often they don't charge a commission, or if they do, it's a flat $7 per trade. In your interview, be sure that if you plan to do a lot of trading, ask what commissions you might pay for trades, as they can add up and reduce your return over the long term.

Also keep in mind that choosing the lowest cost provider overall isn't always the best option, as they might not offer the necessary level of service or advice. For instance, my firm provides financial planning in addition to investment planning, which requires more time and expertise, and thus, we aren't the most inexpensive firm out there. At the same time, we're not the most expensive. Comparing providers that align with your require-ments is vital before making a final decision.

7. What investment philosophy do you follow?

What you are looking for here is the investment philosophy the advisor and their firm subscribe to. Do they believe in active management or passive management? Do they believe they can outperform the market, or do they believe that using low-cost index funds is a better approach? I personally embrace the core principle of using low-cost passive investment strategies, not high-cost active strategies. Investment costs have a large impact on a portfolio's long-term growth, and you want your advisor to strive to keep those costs to a minimum, as well as keep your portfolio risk in line with your risk tolerance.

As an example, our investment process begins with completing a Retirement Readiness Report for each client. After this analysis, we determine the asset allocation (mix of stock and bond funds) that best fits our clients' needs.

I recommend you ask to see a sample of what the advisor you're considering would invest in for you. If their recommended portfolio consists mainly of high-cost mutual funds, I would steer clear of working with them and seek out an advisor who embraces the lower-cost strategies mentioned above.

As a final note, many people associate low cost with poor quality. For instance, if you're considering buying two pairs of shoes, one for $100 and the other for $25, you'd assume that the $25 pair would likely wear out faster than the $100 pair. With tangible products, you generally do get what you pay for. However, when it comes to investment products, the opposite is often true. Competition among investment providers has, over time, significantly reduced the fees charged for investment products, which means those lower costs are passed on to you as the client.

8. Where do you keep my money and how can I see it?

You've likely heard of Ponzi schemes, such as Bernie Madoff's, that left his clients stripped of their savings. To ensure this never happens to you, the advisor you hire should recommend that your investments be held by an independent third party, known as a custodian, rather than by the advisor directly—and tell you which custodian they use. Your advisor should help you open any accounts at that custodian, after which you give limited authorization to your advisor to trade the accounts and collect the management fee from them. In my firm, to protect our clients, every other transaction requires their authorization.

Your advisor should also inform you of how you'll be able to check on your accounts at any given time. It is your right to see what your money is doing, and a good advisor will use a custodian who makes your accounts accessible to you as a client, either through statements, online, or both. In my firm, we also subscribe to third-party performance software called Orion, which not only allows us to generate quarterly investment performance reports, but also hosts a website where our clients can check investment performance at any time.

9. How, and how often, will we communicate?

As I mentioned, in-person meetings are not a prerequisite for hiring your ideal advisor, as video-conferencing is an option for most every advisor today. You'll want to find out if an initial in-person meeting to go over all of your assets and goals is required, or if the advisor is fine with evaluating your financial documents via Dropbox, WeTransfer, email, or a proprietary document transfer system, if that's more feasible for you.

Then, you'll want to ask about ongoing communication. In my firm, for example, we recommend meeting with our clients either in person or via video conference at least two times during the year. These meetings occur in the early spring (March/April) and the late fall (October/November). We have found these times work best to review client asset allocations, make ongoing updates to financial plans, and address any tax planning opportunities. If something comes up between these scheduled meetings, we will reach out to the client. We are also available for additional meetings and phone calls when requested.

You may also want to ask if they provide a weekly, biweekly, or monthly market commentary email, to keep clients updated on what's going on in the financial markets and to identify any planning opportunities. In addition, you may want to ask if the firm conducts any client education events on various financial topics, or if the advisor has a podcast, writes a blog, or hosts a YouTube channel, if education is important to you.

10. How long has your longest client been with you, and how many clients do you advise?

The first part of this question will give you an idea of the advisor's client longevity and loyalty. If they still work with many of their original clients, that is a good sign. Of course, an advisor can claim untruths here and it might be difficult to prove otherwise. In the best-case scenario, however, a competent and trustworthy advisor will have at least a few clients who may be willing to speak to a potential client, to give a testimonial about how that advisor operates. (Note that until 2022, client testimonials were not allowed on advisors' websites, so expect to find none or very few.) Though you can't necessarily prove the contact given to you is an authentic client of the advisor, it is still within your right to ask, and the advisor should have no problem obliging.

The second part of the question gives you a sense of how heavy the client load may be, in terms of how much attention is feasibly given to each client. If the advisor has a team in his or her firm, they will obviously handle more clients than an individual would. I, for example, currently advise roughly one hundred families and am still accepting new clients. My goal is always to be the last financial advisor my clients will ever need, and I want you to find that same commitment in the advisor you ultimately hire.

I like the round number of ten for the top questions to ask, but there is one more question I've come to believe is as important as the previous ten:

11. What ongoing education do you participate in?

This question will hopefully elicit a multitude of answers, as there are a multitude of ways for an advisor to participate in ongoing education. In fact, a financial advisor is obligated to stay up to date with what's occurring in the financial market, and should therefore be committed to being a lifelong learner. There is never a point of being able to say, "I already know what I need to know." Tax laws constantly change and investment strategies fluctuate; exploring new opportunities to take advantage of some of these changes and minimize taxes for you as a client is imperative. In addition, certain ongoing education is mandatory. As a fee-only financial advisor, as mentioned prior, thirty hours every two years is required to maintain the basic licenses alone.

Here are some of the ways your prospective financial advisor should express staying current in the industry:

- ✦ Keeping up with tax changes, such as regulations around when clients have to take money out of their retirement accounts, the required minimum distribution age, etc. For example, in early 2020, Congress came out with the SECURE Act, which introduced several changes to tax laws and retirement accounts. Just when advisors and clients were getting comfortable with those changes, in 2022 Congress

introduced the SECURE Act 2.0, with even more
changes than the SECURE Act 1.0.

+ Reading books, blogs, newsletters, and financial reports

+ Attending webinars, live in-person trainings, and
conferences

+ Obtaining education in areas where the advisor may be
deficient, or in niche areas that would further help their
clients make even more profitable investments, such as
tax planning, insurance planning, estate planning, and
the like

+ Listening to credible podcasts

+ Studying behavioral patterns that can influence clients
to sometimes do the wrong thing at the wrong time, due
to their emotional wiring

+ Enrolling in ongoing courses on niche topics, such as
Social Security or Medicare, to name two, because
regulations change and the refreshers are helpful, as it
can be challenging to remember all the details over time

———

Once you have conducted your interview and received favorable
answers to all of these questions, you want to check in with your
gut. What is it telling you? Do you feel a sense of trust and com-
patibility with this advisor? Do your personalities meld well?
After all, this is a valuable relationship you intend to maintain
for many years, so you want to enjoy communicating with this
person. Like a doctor who may be competent in their field but

not have the best bedside manner, you could meet with an excellent financial advisor but their "bedside manner" is lacking. If this is the case, I recommend that you continue conducting interviews until you've found the ideal match in competency *and* personality. This end-to-end alignment will help to ensure that you don't avoid communication with your advisor, which won't be beneficial to you in the long run.

The good news is, most financial advisors have a retention rate of 90 percent. Once people choose their advisor, they don't typically leave unless there are trust or investment performance issues that call the advisor's capability or ethics into question.

In the next chapter, we'll touch on what you can expect from the financial advisor you've chosen to hire, so that you can adequately prepare for the first meeting of your partnership, as well as how you can help to ensure a long and prosperous relationship.

4

I'VE HIRED MY ADVISOR, NOW WHAT?

How to Prepare for and What to Expect from Your Partnership

———•———

After you have done all the essential work of evaluating and choosing your ideal financial advisor—one who can deliver on your particular needs of planning and/or investing—you will need to know how that partnership is established, what materials you need to provide to your new advisor, and what to expect in your relationship going forward in terms of ongoing communication and support. In this chapter, we will outline all of these, with the goal of replacing any overwhelm or anxiousness you may feel with abundant ease and confidence.

YOUR INITIAL MEETING WITH YOUR NEW FINANCIAL ADVISOR

Once you've decided on the financial advisor you want to hire, you will need to enter into a contract with them for the services you'll be receiving. If they will be providing **investment manage-**

ment, you'll need to sign their investment management agreement. If they will be providing **financial planning** only, you'll need to sign their financial planning agreement and pay them the upfront fee required to begin the assessment of your documents and the crafting of your financial plan. There is one set of protocols for investment management and another for financial planning only. If your advisor will be providing both investment management and financial planning combined—often referred to as **wealth management**—the protocols will often overlap. I will cover both of these processes in detail as we go through this chapter.

Investment Management Onboarding

If your advisor will be providing you with investment management services only, or investment management and financial planning, they will often begin your relationship by first addressing your investment accounts. This entails signing your investment management agreement and agreeing to their investment management fee schedule. It is crucial that you agree to this and understand the fees you'll be paying for this service.

Next, your advisor will help you open investment accounts with the custodian (company that holds your money) or broker they use. For example, we primarily work with Charles Schwab as our custodian and therefore assist our clients in opening new accounts there. If they have existing accounts with Charles Schwab, we are sometimes able to be added to those accounts, eliminating the need to open new ones.

The next step is helping you transfer your existing investments into your new investment account(s). This could be done through electronic transfers known as ACATs or DTC. Some transfers may involve you calling your previous investment company and requesting paperwork to transfer your accounts.

If you have retirement plans with previous employers, you may need to reach out to them to find out how to transfer this money, or request a rollover of the funds if your advisor believes it is in your best interest to do so. If all goes smoothly, this account opening and transfer process is typically completed within a few weeks, longer if there are issues with paperwork or with transferring accounts.

Once all of your investments have been transferred to your new advisor, you'll want to have them review the portfolio and decide upon your new investment strategy. This is a good time to sign an investment policy statement that lays out your new strategy and expectations going forward. I'll address investment policy statements in greater detail in Chapter 6.

If your new advisor will also be providing financial planning advice, this is commonly the next step, now that your investment portfolio is established. If they won't be providing financial planning advice, you will schedule a follow-up meeting with your advisor, usually one to two months after your accounts have been transferred. This is so you can confirm that everything has been transferred and to address any questions you may have with your new account statements.

Your Engagement Proposal / Scope of Work for Financial Planning

In Chapter 2, I gave you a list of potential needs that an advisor could assist you with. For ease of reference, I have provided them again:

- cash flow management / budgeting
- investment strategies
- ongoing investment management
- planning and/or investing for a new child / current children
- planning and/or investing for a wedding and new life as a couple
- dealing with financial situations surrounding a divorce
- buying or selling a home
- planning for college
- planning for retirement
- dealing with financial situations surrounding the loss of a spouse
- inheritance of a large sum of money
- buying, starting, or selling a business
- analyzing tax returns and collaborating with your accountant
- guidance on insurance
- guidance on taxation, in general
- guidance on estate planning
- guidance on wills and trusts

In a financial planning only partnership, you must both define the relationship by agreeing on the "scope of work" or "scope of engagement," which will incorporate your needs from above. Your advisor should provide you with this scope of work in writing. This will ensure that all of your planning needs are addressed, and that your advisor will be delivering on all of your requirements. Prior to signing this scope of engagement, you'll want to make any necessary changes to it.

The scope of engagement should include the following:

+ What areas of your financial plan will your engagement cover? Will it be a limited engagement and cover one area such as your investments, or will it be a comprehensive review?

+ Are you going to be responsible for implementing the recommended plan on your own, or is your advisor going to help you implement it?

+ What is the timeline for completing the financial plan? How often will you be meeting with your advisor?

+ Are they going to give you written recommendations?

Note here that implementation is often the most difficult part. This will typically require you to make changes to your budget, insurance coverages, tax strategies, estate plan, and possibly more. If you can have your advisor help you with this, you're more likely to follow through with their advice and not miss anything. Do note, however, that this level of assistance will likely incur an additional cost because more of the advisor's time will be involved.

Checklist of Basics

Besides your personal information—if you're married or part-nered, have children or plan to, care for an ill parent or family member, your employer or business from which you receive your income, etc.—your advisor will require additional information and personal financial documents to begin working on your financial plan. Here are some of the documents you will likely need to provide:

- ✦ Your last two years of tax returns
- ✦ A statement of net worth (for a sample, see https://www.morrisseywealthmanagement.com/free-resources)
- ✦ A pay stub, if you have an employer, or a YTD Quickbooks report, if you are self-employed or run a small business
- ✦ Your investment statements, if you have any
- ✦ Contact information for any other members of your current financial team (financial advisor, accountant, insurance agent, stockbroker, estate planning attorney)

Additional Materials

Budget Worksheet

In my firm, and in most others, you will be asked to complete a budget worksheet. For this, you will need to assess all of your typical monthly expenses, and if you are retiring soon, account for any changes in your budget due to retirement. We use a fillable Excel worksheet (see https://www.morrisseywealthmanagement.com/free-resources). Other firms may use something similar.

Insurance

If you hold a life insurance policy, or any disability or long-term care insurance, you will want to have these policies to share with your advisor. If you don't have these policies in place, your fiduciary advisor may recommend them for you, but they will not have a license to sell you these products (remember, we don't want an advisor who receives commissions!). In this case, they will ensure you are not unnecessarily spending money on insurance premiums you don't need.

Here's but one example of an insurance recommendation:

> You may have disability insurance, but it's a low monthly coverage amount because you purchased it a while ago when your salary was lower. If needed, it would only cover 20 percent of your pre-disability income. Having analyzed your situation, your advisor sees that you could now be insured for up to 60 percent of your pre-disability income—income your family would need in the event you became disabled.

Estate Planning Documents

If you already have a will or trust, you will want to have a copy for your advisor. He or she will also want to know:

✦ Do you have final instructions written to your executor about burial wishes, where they can find your assets, who your trusted advisors are, and any special requests for items not included in your will? This is sometimes called a "Love Letter to My Family." An example can be

found on my website at: https://
www.morrisseywealthmanagement.com/free-resources.

✦ Do you have important ancillary documents, like a
healthcare power of attorney and/or financial power of
attorney?

✦ Are your beneficiaries listed correctly on retirement
accounts and life insurance policies? (You'd be surprised
how often people don't have contingent beneficiaries
listed. This could significantly increase the cost to settle
your estate and cause delays).

YOUR RECOMMENDED FINANCIAL PLAN

Once your advisor has all your documentation and is clear on
your goals, he or she will begin to analyze the data you've provided and present recommendations for your financial plan.
This is usually not a one-and-done plan, as there are many options
to achieve your goals, and those goals may be interconnected.
As such, you will go through the process of deciding which
goals are the most important to you. Once you've decided on
which goals to pursue, your advisor will develop your recommendations.

To give you an idea of how this may work, in our firm this
planning process takes four to six meetings. Ideally, we schedule
an in-person or Zoom meeting with the client every few weeks
once we begin the process. We start with the retirement planning
analysis meeting, as this goal has the most variability: dates someone can choose to retire, options for collecting Social Security, etc.

Once we've addressed retirement planning, we move on to

investment planning, then tax planning, then insurance planning, then wrap up with estate planning. (Each of these is expanded on individually in Chapter 5, except for investment planning, which is the focus of Chapter 6.) If the client will not be engaging us for investment management, we will nonetheless review their investments and make recommendations.

To assist in the planning process, many financial advisors and planners use dedicated software. This is not a requirement, however; if your advisor is a whiz with Excel, they can complete your financial analysis on that platform. If they do use financial planning software, the two most popular are Emoney and MoneyGuide Pro. We use Emoney because it is cash-flow based, and we believe cash-flow planning is essential to any analysis.

The benefit of using software like Emoney is that it can generate hundreds of useful reports; the drawback is that it can make your financial plan over one hundred pages in length. In the beginning of my career, I would present the full report to my clients, and I'd often receive a blank stare and the question: "What am I supposed to do with this?" So, I began to highlight and summarize the most important parts. Still, that chunk of paper was overwhelming because they had to thumb through all of it to find the highlights.

That's when I realized that clients needed an executive summary. For a while, I created a summary that was two or three pages long—until I stumbled upon a colleague who coined the term "one-page plan." He took every pertinent piece of information for the client's financial plan and fit it onto a single page (at times a double-sided page, but still one page). This is what I've done for my clients—and what I recommend of your advisor— for many years now, and I can say that it changes the game for you as a client. You don't need to drag yourself through a stack of massive reports; if your advisor hands this to you, they're doing you a disservice. It is their job to simplify a process that can be complicated. In our firm, for example, we keep the extended report in a binder we can reference for how everything is calculated, but a concise report is all you need as a client. You're much more likely to understand and follow your plan if you have it on one page versus a hundred-page document.

With plan and recommendations in hand, you will then begin the somewhat challenging task of implementing the recommendations. I say challenging because this is something you can't often implement in one meeting. Also, depending on the financial planning agreement you have, your advisor may or may not help you with the implementation. For example, they may recommend you reallocate your 401(k). You could either do this on your own, or if you have an agreement for assistance with implementation, your advisor could walk you through how to accomplish this through a screen-sharing session.

Overall, a good advisor will follow up and hold you accountable in implementing your recommendations. In part this is vital because failing to implement your advisor's recommendations can have devastating effects for your financial plan and your family. (See examples of this in Chapter 5.)

While I strive to help my clients be accountable to the tasks I give them, in the end it is your responsibility as a client to ensure you complete those tasks in a timely manner. And if you are in the later stages of life, that time may be even more precious. You want to feel peace of mind about what will happen to your estate, how your finances will be handled, and what responsibilities your family will be left with, whether or not you have a large inheritance to leave behind. Of course, those with more substantial estates and assets to allocate will require more time to complete all the steps involved, but either way, once the tasks are complete, you can live worry-free knowing that piece of your financial life is in place and that you've made all the decisions that mean the most to you for after you're gone.

COORDINATION WITH OTHER ADVISORS AND FOLLOW THROUGH

If you have come into the partnership with other members already on your team—another financial advisor, an accountant, an attorney, etc.—you will have provided your new advisor with their names, roles they play for you, and contact information, as already mentioned. Your new advisor, with your permission, will now reach out to each of them to set up a brief meeting. The purpose of this is to discuss your financial plan and how as a team they will form a coordinated effort for your most beneficial results.

HOW OFTEN TO MEET AND/OR COMMUNICATE

We touched on this in Question #9 in the Top Ten Questions list in Chapter 3, but I want to expound on it a bit here, as many people are unclear about how often to be in touch with their advisor and vise versa.

During your initial interview, you will have determined your advisor's review schedule and hopefully confirmed that before signing your agreement. In my firm, for example, for ongoing wealth management clients (investment management clients), we typically meet twice a year. This isn't common across the board, however; I often meet with potential clients who rarely if ever hear from their advisor. I find this unacceptable, as you could be missing valuable tax planning opportunities, so do be sure your advisor is willing to meet with you at least once a year, depending on your needs and agreement.

In preparation for our biannual meeting, I will ask my client two simple questions: "What's new?" and "What's changed?" Similar to the list of reasons we discussed in Chapter 1 for hiring a financial advisor, these are common answers:

+ you changed jobs or received a promotion
+ your company downsized and your position has changed
+ you had another child
+ you had a grandchild
+ you got engaged or married
+ you're getting a divorce
+ you inherited money
+ you're thinking of buying a house
+ you're thinking of buying a second house
+ you're thinking of moving
+ you're thinking of retiring
+ you're considering starting, buying, or selling a business
+ you want to update your estate plan
+ you want to rethink some of your insurance coverage

Any of these life events are typically discussed during our regular meetings, but if one or more of these occur in between, and you feel you need your advisor's immediate attention, you should be able to set up an additional meeting with no problem.

I also prepare for one of our annual meetings by requesting a copy of my client's tax return, which they send electronically. Using tax planning software, I'm able to import that tax return and create scenarios, allowing us to look toward the next year. For example:

> If we determine that you need to earn $80,000 in the coming year from your portfolio, I'll devise the most tax-efficient way to extract that money. We'll then look at what the next three to five years is going to look like and come up with a long-term strategy, aiming to minimize the taxes you'll pay. We'll also look into any tax changes that are slated for the coming year(s) and factor those into your plan as well. This a substantial value-add we can quantify as advisors that can potentially save you money in income taxes by paying taxes at a lower rate.

In assessing any and all changes in your life, your advisor can ensure they're making shifts to your financial plan to facilitate your new goals or circumstances. Your advisor's expertise can be invaluable in this arena: they will assure you're making the best decisions and not putting yourself or your family in an unfavorable position simply because you didn't know what you didn't know.

I have been working with some of my clients for twenty years now, and I'm consistently managing their portfolios and evaluating optimal updates. I also check in with my client's team, if there is one, at least once a year—and anytime there is a significant change—to make certain we are all on the same page for our client. You will want to set forth the same expectations of your financial advisor. If you call and need an answer to a simple question, you should receive a call back within a day or two; if you have a question that may require some research, expect your advisor to need some extra time, but also to give you a timeframe you can count on.

In sum, you should expect and receive:

✦ regularly scheduled annual or biannual meetings
✦ requested meetings between if there is a substantial change or concern
✦ prompt responses to simple questions
✦ realistic timeframes for more complex questions, with follow through as promised

In the best-case scenario, your advisor will strive to practice "underpromising and overdelivering." They will also own up to any mistakes or poor follow-through by being accountable to you. Your advisor may know a lot about various things, but if they don't know the answer to a question, they should tell you they need to find out the correct information instead of simply doling out a stock response that may end up being detrimental to you. It is my belief that the more good you do for people, the more goodwill you create, and the more people will appreciate it. The Golden Rule isn't golden for nothing.

WITHDRAWAL REQUESTS

One last reason you may need to speak to your advisor between meetings is to make a withdrawal from an account. If you find yourself in a situation where you need money, and the only source you can pull from is your investment accounts, you will need to discuss your options with your advisor.

While it may seem like the easiest, least stressful route, here is what you **don't** want to occur:

Your advisor simply says, "Okay," and arbitrarily takes money from one of your accounts and sends it to you.

Your fiduciary should never act in anything but your best interest. If you need a quick infusion of cash, here is what you **do** want to occur:

Your advisor takes the time to have a conversation with you, where you discuss questions such as:

- ✦ What does your income look like for the year?
- ✦ What does it look like for the next three years?
- ✦ If we took this money from different buckets in your portfolio, how could that benefit you?
- ✦ Are there strategies we can use that would save you money in taxes if we took it from one bucket versus another?

This is how fiduciaries add to the value they give to their clients: by always operating with the client's best interest in mind, not simply the easiest or fastest solution to a request.

In the next chapter, we're going to expand on your relationship with your fiduciary advisor by looking more closely at the four biggest elements of planning for your future: **Retirement** planning, **Insurance** planning, **Tax** planning, and **Estate** planning—or what I call Getting It R-I-T-E.

5

GETTING IT
R-I-T-E:

Planning for Your Future —
Retirement, Insurance, Taxes, Estate

———◦———

E ven if you love what you do for a living, if you're like most people, you don't want to do it forever. At some point, you'd probably like to retire, and you'd like to do so with a plan that allows you to live comfortably and do the things you most enjoy. This plan includes carrying only the insurance that makes sense for your life situation, paying the minimum amount of taxes, and having a solid plan for your estate when the time comes to pass it on. This is why I've devoted an entire chapter to "getting it R-I-T-E" in planning for your future. Once these four elements are in place, you can quell your anxiety and feel assured as you move into the next phase of your life.

Many people avoid this planning because it brings up aging and even mortality—two topics most of us don't like to think about. But after twenty-two years as a financial advisor, I can tell you that *not* planning ahead generally causes a great deal more angst than making the effort to do so—and sometimes putting it off can result in scenarios I never want to see anyone face. In short, engaging your financial advisor in planning for your future will not only give you a sense of financial security for yourself, but you'll know you'll be leaving your loved ones in the best financial position possible should something happen to you.

RETIREMENT PLANNING

We'll begin with our "R"—Retirement—by breaking down each aspect of retirement planning into manageable bites. By the end of this section, you should have a strong grasp on what priorities you want to focus on for your particular plan, and hopefully feel confident charting a path in that direction.

Determining Your Retirement Goals

The key to knowing how to plan for your retirement is to know what kind of life you'd like to have. This obviously varies a great deal depending on one's lifestyle, financial position, and family ties. For example:

Do you want to be debt-free and save up a million dollars?

Do you want to be able to go on three nice vacations a year?

Do you want to finally have that second home you've dreamed of?

Do you mostly want to spend time with your children, grandchildren, or friends?

Do you want to help pay for your grandchildren's education or other pursuits of interest?

Do you dream of being a homebody and being happy by simply not having to go to work, doing a lot of relaxing, and maybe dabbling in a few hobbies?

Do you want to spend a lot of time traveling?

Do you want to sell your house and scale down to a smaller one?

Do you want to spend a lot of time volunteering and supporting causes you care about?

Do you want to take up—or expand on—a sport or hobby?

Do you want to become a collector or enthusiast of something you've always loved?

Do you still want to work, but only part-time in a low-stress setting you're drawn to, such as a local museum, school, nursery, or shop?

You may answer yes to a number of these questions, or you may gravitate to only one or two. The point is that you want to weigh all the facets of your life you'd like your retirement years to encompass—keeping in mind that you might go through phases. In other words, you may travel more in your younger retirement years, and take up certain hobbies in later years, for one example. Whatever your aspirations may be, specifying your goals will help your financial advisor chart a path for those goals to be feasible in all stages of your retirement years. That may mean meeting mini goals, annually or quarterly, that are measurable for you. I find that often, having shorter-term goals that lead into longer-term goals encourage my clients to be more accountable and to track their progress.

Planning Your Income

In the simplest terms, retirement planning is financially quantifying what it will require to support your retirement goals. For example:

> If you currently spend $50,000 a year, and you project you're going to spend $50,000 a year in retirement, we must figure out a plan to generate $50,000 a year in income for you. First, we look at what income sources you are eligible for: Social Security is one; a pension may be another. Perhaps you have both, and combined they will provide $30,000 in income a year. That leaves a $20,000 shortfall. If you have ten years before you plan to retire, we would then use a savings calculator to determine how much extra money you need to save each year to provide that extra $20,000 a year.

This is a simplistic way of looking at it, but that is the essence of retirement planning.

Here in the United States, it used to be that most companies took care of your retirement plan for you. Many of them provided a pension, and that pension, combined with Social Security, was sufficient for the majority to retire comfortably. Now, however, pensions are rare and are usually only offered to government and state workers. This elimination of a secondary source of income is one of the reasons it falls on you as an individual to make sure you save enough for retirement.

One of the biggest factors in your retirement plan is the age you begin saving. It goes without saying that the sooner you begin saving, the more time you give your money to benefit from compound growth. Many people don't get serious about planning their retirement until they are 50 to 55, which means the average number of years they have to save for retirement is twelve to fifteen. If, however, you begin planning at 60 with a goal to retire at 65, that lowers your saving window to only five years. Hence, my hope is that you'll benefit from this book no matter your age, but if you happen to be on the younger side of the range, you will reap the greatest benefits of longer-term saving plans.

Another point to note is that if you remain healthy and have decades of quality life ahead of you, Social Security alone will likely not be sustainable for you. It is a decent income for some, but most people require a great deal more, especially if you have some of the loftier goals listed at the beginning of the chapter. Again, saving enough from each paycheck now to supplement your income above and beyond Social Security is the goal.

Early Withdrawals

While the money you've put aside for retirement is yours, and you may have a concrete need to make early withdrawals at times, I do caution you not to exceed the amount you and your advisor have preemptively planned for. Yes, it's your money, and you can do whatever you like with it; however, excessive withdrawals that deplete your retirement funds may leave you in a less-than-favorable position when your retirement age arrives, and I hate to see clients have to work longer than anticipated to replace those lost funds. So, do keep in mind that it's your financial advisor's responsibility to keep you abreast of your financial situation: if they recommend cutting back on withdrawals to avoid running out of money, they are likely doing so with your best interest at heart.

The Three Phases of Retirement

I often work with clients who have done an excellent job of taking care of their children—providing them with a home, education, and opportunities—but they're hesitant to spend money in retirement, fearing they'll leave nothing behind for them. While wanting to leave a legacy for your children is commendable, I believe it's equally essential to enjoy the rewards of a lifetime of hard work.

With this in mind, I encourage you to think about your retirement in three phases: the "go-go years" (the first ten years of your retirement), the "slow-go years" (the next ten), and the "no-go years" (the ten after that).

With proper nutrition, exercise, and mindset, maintaining outstanding health as we age *is* an achievable goal for most of us, despite the constant onslaught of messages telling us to expect declining health simply because we grow older. But in the event you do find yourself less mobile over time, or some things you want to do become more difficult or even impossible to achieve, I recommend focusing on having adventures and creating amazing memories in your go-go years when you're healthy and able. Maybe you've always wanted to take a Mediterranean cruise, or to visit the pyramids in Egypt, or to explore the USA on extended road trips. Sure, this may mean spending more of your money in your go-go years, and therefore less later on, but this way you won't miss out on anything because you've gotten yourself stuck, believing you must spend the same amount each year of your retirement (or close).

Let's take a look at an example.

Say you have $50,000 a year in consistent income planned from age 65 to 95. For those thirty years, that's a total of $1,500,000. If you wanted to keep that total income goal, but allocate more in the first ten years than in the last twenty, your fiduciary could help you determine how to achieve that. Perhaps you could save or invest more for the first ten years, such that your income from 65 to 75 would be $80,000 a year, which would be $800,000 total. That would leave $700,000 for the last twenty years, which would divide into $35,000 a year. If you believe this would be doable in your later years, I recommend getting as much enjoyment out of those first ten as you can. Of course, adjustments could be made in either direction, based on the goals you'd like to bring to fruition.

Spenders vs. Savers

I have found that my clients fall into one of two categories: spenders or savers. The spenders are—no surprise!—comfortable spending their money. I help them devise a spending plan that aligns with their portfolio's performance, and we review that portfolio annually to determine how much money they can comfortably spend. We also look at places they might tend to overspend, and discuss how they can reel themselves in, if need be.

The savers, on the other hand, have typically under-consumed and saved a significant portion of their income their entire life. Despite having a substantial amount of money saved for retirement, they struggle to transition from saver mode to spender mode. During a meeting, I'll say something like, "You spent $60,000 from your portfolio last year, but you could have spent $100,000. What did you do with the extra $40,000?" You guessed it: they saved it! This is when I encourage them to spend more, giving them examples of big purchases they could make or trips they could take with the extra money.

Now, you may think this sounds irresponsible, but I remind these clients that spending money in retirement is not necessarily a bad thing. In fact, it can allow them to achieve a dream or experience items on their bucket lists. As such, I give them a conservative spending estimate and encourage them to enjoy the fruits of their labor while they can. There is no guarantee of what lies ahead, and postponing dreams and aspirations may lead to regret, especially if health concerns or other unexpected issues arise, rendering you unable to do the things you once wished to accomplish.

In the event that your goal is to leave your heirs a significant inheritance, even at the expense of missing out on things you would love to do, that is certainly your prerogative. That monetary gift from you won't go to the government or the tax man, which may make you feel great. And providing for them may give you more joy than anything you might want to do for yourself. But remember that your loved ones may be much happier knowing you didn't make unnecessary sacrifices in your life, merely to leave money behind. With this in mind, there's usually a way to strike a balance, whereby you get to enjoy the money you've so diligently saved while still leaving a significant gift to those you love.

Choosing the Right Age for Retirement

Even if you are independently wealthy, or you've been saving and investing wisely for a long time, lifestyles and expenses tend to grow in relation to assets and income. Hence, it is a rare person today who doesn't have some degree of concern about having enough money as they age. Choosing the right retirement age is crucial to your retirement plan's success for two reasons:

1. At the end of your career, you're likely earning your highest salary yet, and finding another job with similar pay can be difficult.

2. The earlier you retire, the sooner you will need to begin withdrawing from your nest egg, potentially shortening the amount of time it will last. This is why I tell clients to be certain they have run the numbers and will be okay financially if they retire. Very few people get a retirement do-over.

While my hope is that the fiduciary you've hired will guide you responsibly, I've met with older clients whose prior advisors encouraged them to retire too early. These clients began spending from their portfolio, only to discover in their 80s that they were running out of money. Even with their other sources of income, such as Social Security, they wouldn't have enough to cover all their expenses in the years to come.

It's true that it is an individual's responsibility to keep an eye on their portfolio, if for some reason they don't have annual meetings with their advisor. But I also know that at times, some advisors neglect to tell their clients the hard truth. I hope this won't be the case for you, but do let your advisor know you always expect straight answers to tough questions, no matter if they might be hard to hear. You want to cover all your bases with regard to your most advantageous retirement age, and you should be able to count on your advisor to steer you in the best direction.

Social Security

Social Security factors heavily into most people's retirement plan. All Americans who work must pay into the system and are therefore eligible for a benefit.

Your full retirement age benefit is based on the year you were born. While you are eligible to collect your benefits early, beginning at age 62, your benefits will be reduced based on your full retirement age, as outlined in the table below.

Age to receive full Social Security benefits		
Year of Birth[1]	Full Retirement Age	Percent of Full Retirement Benefit Available at Age 62[2]
1943–1954	66	75.00
1955	66 and 2 months	74.16
1956	66 and 4 months	73.34
1957	66 and 6 months	72.50
1958	66 and 8 months	71.67
1959	66 and 10 months	70.83
1960 and later	67	70.00

[1] People born on January 1 of any year refer to the previous year.
[2] Percentages are approximate due to rounding.

Another factor to consider if you collect your Social Security benefits before reaching your full retirement age is that there is a limit to how much you can earn if you hold a job, as shown below.

SOCIAL SECURITY EARNINGS LIMITS

Age	Benefit Reduction	Per Income Earned	Over Annual Income
Age 62 to end of year prior to full retirement age	$1	$2	$22,320[1]
In the year you reach full retirement age	$1	$3	$59,520[1]
Starting with the month you reach full retirement age	$0	–	No limit

[1] 2024 calculations and amounts. Source: Social Security Administration

For example: if you want to retire at 64, collect your Social Security benefits, and work part-time, you'll only be able to earn $22,320 before your Social Security benefits are reduced.

These annual earnings limits for anyone collecting Social Security early are increased slightly each year, due to inflation. They are still quite low, however. This is why most people don't begin collecting their Social Security benefits until they retire.

You can also earn a delayed credit if you wait until you're past your full retirement age to collect your Social Security benefits.

SOCIAL SECURITY DELAYED RETIREMENT CREDITS

Year of Birth[1]	Yearly Rate of Increase[2]
1933–1934	5.5%
1935–1936	6.0%
1937–1938	6.5%
1939–1940	7.0%
1941–1942	7.5%
1943 or later	8.0%

[1] People born on January 1 of any year refer to the previous year.
[2] Percentages are approximate due to rounding.

What this means is that anyone waiting past full retirement age to begin collecting their benefits will earn an 8 percent increase each year. For example, if your full retirement age is 67 and you wait until age 70 to collect your benefits, you will receive a 24 percent increase in funds over your full retirement benefit. Note that this delayed credit increase is on top of any annual COLA (cost of living adjustment) you may receive each year.

Social Security Cost-of-Living Adjustments (COLA)

Year	COLA	Year	COLA	Year	COLA
2014	1.7%	2017	2.0%	2021	5.9%
2015	0.0%	2018	2.8%	2022	8.7%
2016	0.3%	2019	1.6%	2023	3.2%
		2020	1.3%		

For an understanding of how each year's COLA is calculated, the Social Security Act specifies a formula. Each December, the Social Security Administration compares the average of the third-quarter Consumer Price Index for Urban Wage Earners and Clerical Workers (CPI-W) to the previous year's third-quarter average. If there's an increase, it is rounded to the nearest tenth of one percent, which determines the COLA for the upcoming year. If there is no increase, there is no COLA for that year. (The Social Security COLA can never be negative).

Since the passing of the Social Security Act of 1975, COLAs have averaged 2.8 percent. This is the primary reason why delaying collecting your Social Security benefit until full retirement—or even until age 70—is so important. For example:

Let's say your full retirement age is 67, and your full retirement Social Security benefit is $2,800 per month. You can take it as early as 62, but you will only receive 70 percent of your full retirement benefit. Conversely, if you wait until age 70, you will receive a delayed retirement credit of 8 percent per year, for a total increase of 24 percent over your full retirement benefit. It may look something like this:

Age 62 (early): $1960 per month
Age 67 (full): $2800 per month
Age 70 (delayed): $3472 per month

Note that these numbers don't include any COLA you might receive. If granted as in the past, at an average of 2.8 percent per year, your age 70 benefit would increase to $3,771 per month.

While this gives you a solid overview of how these benefits

work, there is more to consider when deciding to collect Social Security that is beyond the scope of this book. For further education on the topic, I encourage you to check out my podcast at www.retirewithryan.com, as I have a number of episodes focused on Social Security. I also encourage you to make sure your financial advisor is well versed in Social Security and explores multiple scenarios to help you make the most of your benefits.

Pensions

If you are eligible for a pension, you'll want to know how it is calculated and the various disbursement options you have. Most pension formulas take into account:

- ✦ The number of years you work for the organization
- ✦ Your highest salary, or an average of your highest three years of salary

It's crucial to know these two calculation factors, as you wouldn't want to retire early and receive a reduction in your pension that could be avoided by working a few more years.

Here's a scenario I once encountered where this was the case:

I met with a 65-year-old woman who had started teaching late in her career and was relying on herself for retirement. Her pension worked in such a way that she received a 2 percent credit for every year she worked, provided she worked for at least twenty years. However, because she had only worked for fifteen years, her credit would be reduced to 1.5 percent per year. As a result, instead of receiving 40 percent of her salary when she retired, she would only receive 22 percent, which would not be a sustainable income for her.

With this information, I was able to make her aware that retiring early wasn't a good plan for her financially. It was a difficult conversation to have, but it was my responsibility to tell her that working those extra five years would almost double her retirement benefit. Had I not done my research, or if I preferred to avoid upsetting my client, I could have simply agreed with her and advised her to retire. This is why it's imperative you have a financial advisor who is truthful and does the proper research for you.

This woman assumed she could retire at 65 and collect Social Security and Medicare. However, in this case, she was much better off working until she was 70. Though she had her heart set on retiring sooner, she was in good health and capable of working five additional years. When she realized she would not only double her pension benefit, but also increase her Social Security payments by over $600 a month, she agreed it was the right decision.

Additionally, many pensions offer different payout options depending on your marital status. Here is an example of what you might be offered:

Pension Payment Options	Monthly Benefit	Survivor Benefit
Single Life Payment	$1,000.00	$0.0
Joint Payment 33% Survivor	$950.00	$313.50
Joint Payment 50% Survivor	$900.00	$450.00
Joint Payment 66% Survivor	$850.00	$561.00
Joint Payment 100% Survivor	$800.00	$800.00

As you can see, the highest monthly benefit is the Single Life Payment. However, this has no survivor benefit. This means that if the spouse who earned the pension dies early in retirement, they will leave their spouse no survivor benefit.

The next highest monthly amount is the 33 percent survivor benefit. This is better than the single payment, but the surviving spouse might not be able to afford their bills if they only receive a third of the full survivor benefit. This was the case for my grandmother.

My grandfather worked as an engineer for the state of Connecticut building highways. He exercised regularly and ate right, and when he retired at age 59, he was in excellent health and believed he would live for decades. His retirement income was comprised of his state pension and Social Security. 401(k)s didn't exist back then, so he had some additional savings and CDs, but nowhere near what people are able to save today in their retirement plans.

Unfortunately, he only lived fifteen more years after retiring. In his last few months of life, he told my grandmother that she would likely need to sell their house and move in with one of their children because of the bad decision he had made with his pension. Fortunately, my grandmother was able to keep her house, but only by significantly cutting back on her expenses. She lived for twenty-seven years after my grandfather's passing.

In retrospect, I wish my grandfather would have received better advice on his pension and chosen the 100 percent survivor benefit. This would have given my grandmother greater income in retirement—and I'm sure it would have made her more comfortable as well.

While most pension income grows with time invested, I once encountered the opposite, which was highly atypical, so I share it here as a cautionary tale in case it may apply to you.

A client of mine had worked for a Fortune 500 company and knew he had a pension, but he had never looked into it. He was about to turn 60, so I told him to get an estimate for taking it now, as well as an estimate for taking it at 65. Oddly enough, we discovered he would receive more money at 60 than he would at 65—the opposite of how most pensions work. Instead of $2,000 per month at 60, he would receive $1,500 per month at 65. Had we not looked into it, he not only would have lost out on $2,000 a month he was entitled to, but he would have received $500 less per month if he'd waited until he was 65. Ultimately, learning about his pension and taking the benefits at 60 instead of 65 provided him over $100,000 in extra income he didn't even know he was entitled to.

Again, for those of you who have a pension, be sure you know how yours is set up and that you understand the payouts. Some people actually have pensions from prior jobs they have no idea exist. They may even have retirement accounts, like 401(k)s and 403(b)s, and not know where they are or what's in them. If this may apply to you, I recommend doing some research to find out what you possess and what may be owed to you. Your fiduciary can then give you guidance on what to do with these accounts, and how to access the funds you've accumulated.

While many people would love to retire by 60 or 65 but can't afford to, I've also worked with clients who have more than enough savings to retire but won't. When I ask them why they're still working, sometimes the answer is, "I just can't retire." For some, their persona is tied up in their job; for others, they've been working so long and collecting a paycheck that they don't know what else they would do. Even armed with all the facts and my telling them they are financially safe to retire, they can't seem to pull the trigger.

Ultimately, while I understand some people feel conflicted about retiring even when they can, I hate to see anyone working longer than they have to—unless they truly love their work—if they don't want to. Though each person must assess their own situation, goals, and dreams in making the decision to retire, I like to remind people that we all have limited time on this Earth; everyone should enjoy their retirement while they're healthy enough to do so.

Implementation

We discussed implementation and follow-through in Chapter 4, but I want to revisit it here in relation to your retirement plan.

Depending on the partnership you have with your financial advisor, you will likely receive some form of assistance with implementing your retirement plan—but remember it's imperative that you are accountable for the tasks he or she gives you. I have clients who receive five recommendations to implement, and by our next meeting they've done all five, while others consistently fail to take action or implement any of my recommendations. This can be due to a busy schedule, a sense of overwhelm, or pure procrastination. Whatever it may be, it's your job as the client to inform your advisor if you need a little more coaching, or explain honestly why you might need a push. Ultimately, the longer you wait to implement the elements of your retirement plan, the less effective it's going to be. And in the worst case, if you never implement your plan, you waste everyone's time and money—and often sacrifice your future peace of mind along with it.

So, do take implementation seriously. Acting on your advisor's recommendations and making the necessary budget and saving shifts is key to a solid retirement plan.

Tips on Saving for Retirement

+ **Automate your savings wherever you can.** You're more likely to stick with saving and investing if you can automate the process. If you're saving, say, $500 a paycheck and you never see it, it will help you "set it and forget it."

+ **Hold yourself accountable.** If you have a goal to save X amount of money each year, make it a priority. You'll feel great about holding to your promise, and you'll receive the benefit of compound interest as well. You don't want to have to make up for a year's lost savings (or more), so stay on track and keep yourself accountable to your goals.

+ **Take advantage of tax deductions.** There's a high chance you'll be in a lower tax bracket during retirement, so you're better off taking deductions now, which also allows more of your money to grow. One of the biggest deductions is contributing to your retirement plan on a pre-tax basis. (Do note that taking money out of your accounts during retirement will make it taxable.) This is especially beneficial if you currently live in a state with income tax but will be moving to a state with no income tax. Any money you contribute to a retirement account on a pretax basis will then completely avoid state income tax. You may also save on taxes if the state you live in doesn't tax pensions, Social Security, or IRA income below a certain threshold. Certain high-tax states, like my home state of Connecticut, are now offering tax breaks for individuals with retirement income (Adjusted Gross Income) below $75,000 and for couples below $100,000.

Example: If you save $10,000 a year, the whole $10,000 will be saved if it's invested before taxes. If you instead pay 25 percent in taxes now, you actually only save $7,500, and it takes time to make up the lost $2,500.

+ **Save 10 percent of your income as a minimum** (depending on your income and lifestyle, you may need to save more), and then as retirement approaches, gradually increase your savings to between 15 and 20 percent.

+ **Take advantage of free financial calculators online** (bankrate.com has some helpful ones). These tools can help you calculate your expenses and estimate the amount of money you'll receive from Social Security and/or a pension.

INSURANCE PLANNING

The "I" in planning for your future is insurance. As we discussed at length in Chapter 2 and emphasized again in Chapter 3, working with a financial advisor who has no ties to commission-based sales—such as for insurance, stocks, or investment products—is a given. Luckily, you've already chosen a fiduciary, so this is a non-issue for you.

What, then, is your advisor's role with regard to insurance?

Most of us carry multiple types of insurance: auto, home-owner's, health, disability, life, etc. When these policies renew, typically on an annual basis, it's your opportunity to review them and ensure they are still in line with your needs. Some people, however, take out insurance plans and pay the premiums, but they don't review them on a regular basis. Or if they do review them, they may not realize that the coverage and/or deductibles aren't in their best interest. This is where your financial advisor comes in.

I believe that having the proper insurance coverage is equally important to saving for retirement. Though I don't like to scare clients with worst-case scenarios, having appropriate insurance is crucial should, God forbid, one of these situations occur:

+ You develop a disability and can no longer work, or can't perform the same work you could before your disability, yet you have no disability insurance.

+ You are in a car accident in which you sustain serious injuries, yet your auto and/or health insurance don't provide enough coverage for your hospital stay.

+ The unthinkable occurs and you die before having saved enough for retirement, leaving your family in a precarious position because you never took out appropriate life insurance.

My job as a financial advisor is to look over all your policies and weigh the following:

+ Which insurance policies are offered by your employer (if you have one)? Health insurance? Life insurance? Disability insurance? Typically, employer-based insurance is your best option because they're the least costly. Also, there is generally no underwriting for life and disability insurance, meaning that if you're in poor health, you may be required to pay more for coverage or could be denied coverage. However, if you are in good health, it could be less costly for you to obtain your own life insurance policy. You also have the added benefit of keeping the policy should you leave the company.

+ If what's offered through your employer isn't covering what you need, or if you don't have an employer, what types of individual policies might be beneficial?

+ Are you properly insured for different situations? What would lost income would mean to your family now? What would it mean five years from now?

+ Do you have adequate life insurance? If you were to pass away prematurely, and your family is reliant on your income, how would they manage?

+ Do you have adequate disability insurance? If you were to become disabled, and couldn't perform your job as you used to, had to work for a lower wage, or couldn't work at all, would your coverage be enough to replace your lost income?

+ Do you have adequate liability insurance? In the event of a car accident, or if somebody were to get injured on your property, your auto and homeowner's insurance offers coverage—but is it an appropriate amount? We may need to make adjustments, or we may also want to consider an umbrella policy that supplements your homeowner's and auto for a higher amount. That way, if there was a horrible injury on your property, or a car accident left you or your passengers with serious injuries, such that the treatment and claims exceeded your property and casualty coverage, the umbrella policy would kick in. This would help protect you from lawsuits or claims made against your personal or retirement funds.

+ Do you have, or have the necessity for, long-term care insurance? This is coverage you may want to consider the older and the closer to retirement you get, to cover you in the event you can no longer care for yourself. Everyone wants to stay in their home as long as possible, and most long-term care insurance will cover having someone help care for you at home. In the worst case, if you had to be admitted to a full-time nursing home, it would cover you for that expense as well. Note here that your advisor may find this insurance policy is not worth the cost, especially if you can afford to pay for long-term care out of pocket. Long-term care insurance can be expensive, with premiums ranging from $4,000 to $12,000 a year (depending on the coverage amount), and may not be the best option for everyone.

If you don't currently have some or all of these policies, I realize this list may seem like a lot. I also know that rising insurance costs make carrying all the necessary types of insurance a financial burden for some people. What's important is to determine which policies you can afford and which ones meet your priorities. Again, the role of your fiduciary here is to:

+ go over all of your current policies

+ assess the premiums and coverages to ensure they're in line with your needs and budget

+ consider what policies may be beneficial to take out independently

+ ensure you can afford all of your policies within your financial plan, as well as afford possible premium increases in the future

+ refer you to an appropriate insurance agent if you don't already have one for new coverage you may require

Finally, while insurance products are important, being overinsured can lead to unnecessary spending and negatively impact your capital growth. This is why a good fiduciary will assess all of your policies and make sure you're only paying appropriate premiums for coverage you truly need.

TAX PLANNING

No one likes to talk about the "T" in planning for your future: taxes. The truth is that we are terribly overtaxed, so the very word "tax" tends to bring up negative feelings. The good news is, your financial advisor's role is to help you minimize or defer taxation on your retirement savings and investments, so in this section, we're going to talk about the various opportunities that exist with regard to taxes that can help you save a considerable amount of money.

If you're like most people, you probably don't have a long-term tax plan. You may not think about what your income needs will be from year to year, or how you could devise a game plan to reduce your income tax—but this is where your financial advisor can be an invaluable ally.

Tax planning begins with reviewing your tax return from the previous year, so that we can plan accordingly for the year to come and strategize on a long-term plan to minimize taxes. This includes reviewing:

+ where you're saving money and how you're investing money, as there could be opportunities to take additional deductions or invest your money in a way that's more tax efficient

+ if there are certain accounts or retirement plan contributions we should set up

+ if we should take money out of certain accounts, perhaps due to a projection of lower income for the coming year, in which case it can make sense to withdraw money and pay a lower tax rate

+ if you're capitalizing on maximum 401(k) or retirement plan contributions

+ if you're taking advantage of net unrealized appreciation (NUA) if you own stock in a publicly traded company

+ your HSA (Health Savings Account) contributions

+ your Roth IRA contributions

+ if you're a small business owner, if it makes sense to move from a SIMPLE IRA or SEP IRA to a 401(k) profit-sharing plan

All of these elements can lend to tax savings if handled properly, and each one is important to consider. But perhaps the most influential is the tax bracket you fall into. Let's take a minute to look at numbers, so that you understand how the shift in tax bracket can make a huge difference.

The current US tax brackets start at 10 percent for everyone, then jumps to 12 percent, and then to 22 percent. If you're in retirement, for example, even if you're working part-time, the goal is to keep your income from moving into the 22 percent bracket from the 12 percent, as that 10 percent difference equals substantial tax savings. In reality, that difference is an 83 percent reduction from the 22 percent tax bracket to the 12 percent tax bracket. Put another way, every dollar you earn above the 12 percent tax bracket constitutes an 83 percent increase in the taxes you pay.

I realize your retirement income may be well above the 12 percent tax bracket, so you may not be able to take advantage of these savings, but for others this may be feasible with proper tax and income planning.

Another tax distinction you may not be aware of, but that your financial advisor should have expertise in, is that we have different tax rates for how qualified dividends and long-term capital gains are taxed versus ordinary income, interest, non-qualified dividends, and short-term capital gains. For example:

If your taxable income is above the 12 percent bracket, you pay a 15 percent tax on qualified dividends and long-term capital gains. However, if your taxable income for the year is in the 12 percent tax bracket or below, it's possible to have qualified dividends and long-term capital gains taxed at 0 percent. Wouldn't you like to pay 0 percent federal tax? I know I would! And I love when my clients are able to do the same.

2024 Federal Taxable Income Rates		Ordinary Income (interest, earned income, non-Roth retirement distributions)	Qualified Dividends & Long-Term Capital Gains*
Single	Joint Return		
$0–$11,600	$0–$23,200	10%	0%
$11,601–$47,150	$23,201–$94,300	12%	0%
$47,151–$100,525	$94,301–$201,050	22%	15%
$100,526–$191,950	$201,051–$383,900	24%	15%
$191,951–$243,725	$383,901–$487,450	32%	15%
$243,726–$609,350	$487,451–$731,200	35%	15%
$609,351 or more	$731,201 or more	37%	20% (single: $492,301; joint: $553,851)

* Qualified dividends are from domestic corporations and certain foreign corporations, but don't include dividends from certain preferred stock and most REITs. The current maximum tax rate on long-term capital gains (excluding unrecaptured Section 1250 gain, and gain from sales of collectables and qualifying small business stock) is 20%.

For most people, you will be able to pay less tax on your qualified dividends and long-term capital gains as compared to the tax you would pay on ordinary income, interest, and non-qualified dividends. This preferential tax treatment of qualified dividends and long-term capital gains is why a lot of hedge fund managers pay lower federal taxes than their secretaries. And now that you know how the game is played, you and your advisor can be more cognizant of how you structure your portfolio and your income during retirement.

Let's look at another example:

Take a year when you are unemployed with very little income, or early in your retirement before you begin collecting Social Security or withdrawing money from your retirement accounts. Imagine you have a 0 percent long-term capital gains bucket, and your goal is to only fill it with capital gains. Any ordinary income, retirement account distributions, or interest fills up the bucket first. Once the bucket is filled with this ordinary income, there is no more room for long-term capital gains or dividends to be taxed at 0 percent. Instead, they will be taxed at 15 percent or 20 percent, hence why I suggest realizing capital gains during a year you have little to no income, so you can pay a 0 percent capital gains tax. This is the type of home run someone who knows how to play the tax game can easily hit, yet many advisors aren't actively helping their clients do tax planning, and they and their clients are not aware of this advantage. (Feel free to enlighten your advisor if he or she falls into this category!)

At this point, you may be asking why your CPA (Certified Public Accountant) has likely never given you this advice, or mentioned it to you at all. This is because the majority of CPAs don't do tax planning. Why? Because it's simply not how their businesses are designed. Unfortunately, their position is more about reporting the facts after they happen. For example, you gather your tax documents at the end of the year, have an appointment with your CPA, and they plug in all your numbers. They may occasionally make a comment like, "Hey, you could have done this differently." But it's too late because the tax year is already over. While there may still be time to make a couple of contributions to retirement accounts, or to add a few small deductions, the concrete planning we're talking about with regard to your income and where it comes from is already done.

The bottom line is, a CPA can be a valuable asset, but most CPAs and tax professionals don't meet with you at the beginning of the year to talk about where your income is going to come from that year, and what you can do, if anything, to structure how to pay fewer taxes. If your CPA possesses the expertise and it's an option, you may benefit from an arrangement where your CPA meets with you a few times a year to help you with your tax planning. You would pay them an additional fee for this type of advice, but if they're assisting you with sound tax planning, it should be more than worth the cost.

If your CPA doesn't offer this service, or you now realize you've chosen a financial advisor who isn't educated in assisting you with taxes, I suggest seeking out a CPA or financial advisor who does, as the consequences of *not* having this guidance can be substantial. One example of this follows:

I once met with a prospective client, and in going over his most recent tax returns and income, I discovered he had missed out on a $50,000 tax deduction he could have taken. The client's current advisor, who worked for a large, well-known firm, never brought it up, and that omission cost the client 38 percent in taxes—$19,000— between federal and state.

Unfortunately for this client, it was too late for him to correct the mistake, as the tax year was already over. He ended up firing his advisor and hiring my firm to prevent costly tax mistakes like this from happening again. To add insult to injury, he was paying his advisor a fee well above the norm, and the performance of his portfolio had underperformed the stock market by 3 percent a year over the previous five years. This "advisor" was clearly selling garbage to this client—and I cringe to think of the damage he was causing his other clients too.

In sum, financial advisors who are knowledgeable in taxes and tax planning are an invaluable asset to you. This is why we include "analyzing tax returns and collaborating with your accountant" as well as "guidance on taxation" in our list of common needs in Chapter 3. It's also why it's included in Question #4 in our Top Ten list. Yes, your CPA may be an excellent tax planner for you, but your financial advisor—provided they have true expertise in this arena—is in an even better position to help you with taxes. This is because they are managing your investment accounts and can see information such as unrealized capital gains in real time, which gives you a worthwhile advantage on savings opportunities.

ESTATE PLANNING

We've reached the "E" of our Getting It R-I-T-E formula in planning for your future, and that's planning your estate. I know, thinking about your own mortality can be daunting, and many of us would rather put it off than thoughtfully address it. But as I said at the beginning of the chapter: *not* planning ahead generally causes a great deal more angst than making the effort to do so— and sometimes putting it off can result in scenarios I never want to see anyone face.

So, in this final segment of the chapter, we're going to discuss putting all the elements of your estate in place that will give you a sense of financial security for yourself, as well as the peace of mind in knowing you'll be leaving your loved ones in the best financial position possible when or if something happens to you.

For most people, estate planning is about making sure you have control over your estate, and setting it up so that your assets go to your family, friends, charities, etc., in an efficient manner. This also makes the settlement of your estate easier for your loved ones, expediting the process and minimizing unnecessary costs, such as fees paid to advisors, attorneys, or probate courts. Some fees may be unavoidable, but many others can be avoided with proper planning.

If you work with a qualified attorney or financial advisor, the planning of your estate typically takes only one to three months. If necessity calls for it, you can rush the process and complete it within a few days using online estate planning services like legalzoom.com or wills.com, but keep in mind that drafting legal documents will take more time. You may want to engage a reputable attorney to help you with your estate plan, as mistakes in this arena can be costly. However, some of your estate planning can be done without an attorney.

The following steps will guide you on the order and specific tasks involved in planning your estate, in the hope of assuaging any anxiety you may feel and making it as clear and easy as possible.

1. Document Your Intentions

The first thing you will need to do is craft your "Love Letter to My Family." (Once again, you can download a template on my website at: https://www.morrisseywealthmanagement.com/free-resources) This is, on average, an eight-page document that provides various categories for you to fill in with regard to your wishes. When you're finished, you'll want to share it with your family, let them know where it will be located (a fire-safe and waterproof box is an excellent investment if you plan to keep it in your house), and tell them who your trusted advisor(s) will be. It also details who they should reach out to in the event of your death as well as any additional instructions you have for them.

2. Choose Your Executor

This is the person you entrust to handle the settling of your estate, distribution of inheritances, closing of accounts, and any other legal or financial matters. Typically, this will be your spouse, one of your children, a trusted friend, or another family member who is responsible and capable of dealing with what can be an overwhelming task during a difficult time. Should you not have a trusted relative or friend to appoint, you can hire an attorney to be your executor.

Once you've chosen this person, you will want to inform them of your decision, and let them know where your Love Letter to the Family is located so they can carry out your wishes. Some people prefer to keep their wishes private until their passing, but if you want to share the letter with them, that is certainly your prerogative.

3. Write Your Will

If you have not already made a will, it is imperative that you do so now. This is the cornerstone of your estate, and the document that legally dictates where your assets will go. You can draw up a will with an attorney, or you can create one yourself through legalzoom.com or wills.com. If you choose the do-it-yourself route, you will need to have it notarized to make it official. Both options are viable, depending on the level of advice you require, but as your net worth grows, it is worth the extra cost to have an attorney assist with your will.

Once your will is finalized, be sure to keep the original copy in a safe place, and let your executor know where that is, as the original is often required for submission when probate proceedings are necessary. If the original can't be located, it typically complicates and delays the settlement of your estate. I therefore recommend giving your executor and beneficiaries a copy of your will, in the event the original is lost.

It's critical to understand that the absence of a will at the time of your death can be tragic and complicated for those left behind. If you die without a will, your estate will almost always have to go through probate. The probate laws of your state will then dictate how the assets are handed out. The process can drag out for a minimum of nine months, as well as make your estate contestable, causing further delays. In families where there is division or animosity, this can make your loss even more divisive and problematic. And in extreme cases, where previously unknown relatives could exist, any number of awkward situations can result. In one such case:

> A man I knew of died without a will, believing that his estate would be handled via probate. His only living family members were a niece and nephew, and probate law dictated that these two relatives inherit the entire estate. This might have worked out fine except that this man had taken a DNA test to explore his bloodline, and just before he passed away, a distant relative in Germany discovered their connection and realized he had a great-uncle who was alive. Sadly, the man died before finding out he had a great-nephew. As his estate was in probate and soon to be settled, the great-nephew came forward to claim part of the estate. This wasn't a vindictive man; he was actually elated to learn this uncle had survived. During the Holocaust, he was thought to have died, but he had actually escaped to the United States, with no one in his family ever knowing he had lived. Because he hadn't done the simple task of setting up a will, however, his estate ended up in turmoil. Even though he had never met this great-nephew, the young German man was able to make a claim on his $20 million estate because he was a living relative.

While this may be an unconventional example, these kinds of tumultuous scenarios happen all the time when decedents don't leave a will.

Another crucial aspect of your will is if you have minor children. In this case, you will need to name a guardian in the event you pass away and your children are still minors. Special-needs children may require specific provisions as well, such as long-term care or qualification for Medicaid.

4. Prepare Your Ancillary Documents

Two documents you will want to have in addition to your will are a **healthcare power of attorney** and a **financial power of attorney**. The healthcare power of attorney allows someone you trust (often a spouse, family member, or close friend) to make decisions with regard to your health in conjunction with **medical** professionals if you can't make those decisions yourself. The financial power of attorney allows someone you trust (also often a spouse, family member, or close friend) to make **financial** decisions on your behalf if you can't make those decisions yourself. You can give the same person this power of attorney, or you can choose two different people. Either way, these documents are vital for everyone, as without these documents you would need a court order to appoint someone to these positions.

Last, but certainly not least, you need to name all of your beneficiaries and distinguish what each one is entitled to inherit. We will talk more about beneficiaries in detail below.

Once your will is finalized, you want to be sure to review it every few years. You may have beneficiaries to add, such as new children or grandchildren, or you may have changes to make with regard to your executor, beneficiaries, powers of attorney, or allocation of funds.

5. Name Your Beneficiaries

Whom you choose to inherit from your estate can range from a single person to a large number of inheritors. The decision is highly personal and completely up to you. Your inheritors may know ahead of time what they stand to gain from your will, or you may keep all of that information private until you're gone. Only you can know what is appropriate for your particular situation.

Typical inheritors are:

+ spouse/partner
+ children and grandchildren
+ siblings
+ nieces and nephews
+ close friends
+ long-time employees or service providers
+ charitable organizations
+ animal shelters / animal welfare organizations
+ and/or sanctuaries
+ religious affiliations
+ advocacy organizations (environment, clean water, animal rights, organic farming, etc.)
+ alma mater, educational institutions
+ veterans organizations

While it's not my place to guide anyone on how they divide their estate and to whom, I do recommend taking thoughtful care in making your choices, and discussing certain assets with your loved ones so that you can avoid as much potential hurt, shock, or division as possible when your will is read.

If, for just one example, you have two children who would love your vintage baseball card collection, I suggest talking to them about it ahead of time and striving to find either an equitable way of dividing it or willing it as a shared asset. For larger entities like multiple houses, a fair division of monetary value may be your priority, or perhaps one of your children would much rather inherit your small country cabin instead of the larger family home. Again, only you know your family and what dispersing the various items in your estate may mean to specific individuals versus others.

As a reference, your estate is typically comprised of:

+ liquid assets = the money in your bank accounts, retirement account, and/or investment accounts

+ property = one or more homes or land

+ illiquid assets = business interests

+ material belongings = jewelry, furniture, dishes/china, silverware, books, appliances, clothing, electronic devices, musical instruments, tools, photos, etc.

+ collections = coins, stamps, ephemera, dolls, sports memorabilia, music, etc.

+ vehicles = automobiles and/or other recreational vehicles, such as boats or trailers

Once you have chosen your beneficiaries and made clear what each of them will inherit, again you want to review it every few years so that any additions, deletions, or changes that have come about are made official in your will. Take this cautionary tale:

> I once heard about a client who got divorced but never updated the beneficiary form on his retirement account. He remarried and soon after passed away, leaving his ex-wife named as the beneficiary of his half-a-million-dollar retirement account. His current wife sued the ex-wife to claim the account, but there was no recourse for her. This is because courts are unlikely to overturn a beneficiary designation in a situation where it's presumed the decedent established the designation with full mental capacity.
>
> In this case, even though this client had failed to update the beneficiary designation, resulting in unintended consequences, it was concluded that it was the husband's intended outcome to leave that account to his ex-wife.

Apart from your will, be sure you have also put in writing your beneficiaries for insurance policies and investment/retirement accounts—and be sure that these beneficiaries are people or organizations, *not* your estate. Let me explain.

Naming an estate as the beneficiary of a retirement account, especially if a client has a spouse or children they would like to inherit it, can subject the account to creditor claims, probate fees, attorney fees, and income taxes, and it can cause delays in the beneficiaries' inheritance of the account. Case in point:

I once had a client pass away unexpectedly, and when his wife went to file a claim on a retirement account outside of our management, she received the unfortunate news that he had named his estate as the sole beneficiary on that particular account. We had discussed this account a few times, and he was certain his wife was named as the primary beneficiary. Unfortunately, he had been wrong.

His wife was now burdened with opening an estate for her husband and hiring an attorney to settle it. If he had simply named her as the beneficiary on this account, this would have been avoided. To make matters worse, he had significant credit debt when he died, so the credit card companies were able to make a claim against the estate. In addition, she had to cash in this retirement account and pay tax on the money, as she could not roll it over to her IRA.

All told, nearly 50 percent of this account was lost to creditors, probate fees, taxes, and attorney fees, and I felt horrible that she had to go through such turmoil after just losing her husband. This is why I believe financial advisors should ensure that their clients have updated beneficiary designations on all accounts, not only those managed by the advisor.

In the same vein, retirement accounts are individual assets. A married couple can't have a retirement account as joint tenants with rights of survivorship, meaning if one tenant passes away, the other takes over the account. However, they *can* name their spouse as the beneficiary of these retirement accounts. I recommend this for naming a primary beneficiary, with children named as contingent beneficiaries.

Joint Ownership and Transfer on Death

For most married couples, it simplifies the probate process if you keep non-retirement investment accounts, bank accounts, and real estate jointly owned. The most common distinction is Joint Tenants with Rights of Survivorship (JTWROS). This means that both tenants have equal access to the account; upon one of the tenant's passing, the remaining assets can be moved into the other tenant's name.

The major drawback of this type of account is that either tenant can withdraw all funds from the account. For example, if you had a disagreement with your spouse, and he or she wanted to take all the money from your joint tenant account, they could do so. This often happens in the case of a messy divorce or financial fraud, where a person makes a child a joint tenant on their account.

To limit access to your account while you're alive, but also simplify the probate process, you can set up what's known as a TOD (transfer on death) or POD (payable on death) account. This is akin to adding a beneficiary to a non-retirement account. What it means is that while you're alive, only you have access to make withdrawals from this account; upon your death, the assets will be distributed to the beneficiary's name on the account. In this case, probate court will not be involved in the settlement of the account.

If you and your spouse want to keep your finances separate but simplify your estate settlement process, I highly recommend this type of account. Upon your passing, the TOD beneficiary only needs to submit your death certificate and complete some paperwork to transfer the account into their name.

6. Consider Setting Up a Trust

Depending on the value of your estate and how much control you would like to have over it, you may want to consider establishing a trust. A will and a trust do have some overlap, but they are not interchangeable. So, depending on your situation, you may opt to have both. In essence, both wills and trusts provide a means to determine who will receive your assets, but they do so in varying ways, and each has its own advantages and disadvantages.

One of the distinguishing aspects between the two is in how and when they take effect. Wills and revocable trusts don't go into effect until you pass away, whereas an *irrevocable* trust is effective as soon as you sign and fund it. In brief:

A **will** is a "simpler" document than a trust that allows you to:

+ name guardians for children and pets
+ designate where you want your assets to go

A **trust** is a bit more complicated and costly than a will but can provide some solid benefits, such as:

+ offering greater control over when and how your assets are distributed
+ applying to any assets you hold inside the trust
+ being available in various forms and types

- ✦ being used to minimize or avoid probate entirely
- ✦ enabling assets to be pulled from it while you're living, allowing your family to enjoy some of the benefits now rather than later
- ✦ providing asset protection for your beneficiaries

A trust may also be right for you if you want to establish some type of gifting program, either to family members or friends, or to charitable organizations. As of 2024, you can gift $18,000 per person per year without worrying about a gift tax. If you and your spouse are both living, for example, you can each gift a child (or other loved one) $18,000. Beyond that, you begin to impact your lifetime gift allowance; however, that number is currently $13,610,000, so the majority of people will never reach that limit. In short, you have the choice during your lifetime to use some of that exemption by gifting, to use the maximum (if applicable) when you pass away, or a combination of the two.

In sum, when it comes to wills and trusts, one is not necessarily "better" than the other, only more appropriate for your particular circumstance. Be prepared to present your goals and needs to your financial advisor, and he or she will explain the details of both, help you weigh all the options, and decide on the solution that best suits and protects your family.

7. Discuss Estate Taxes

When I first started in the business twenty-two years ago, the most important aspect of estate planning was minimizing the estate tax. At the time, there was a relatively low valuation for an estate to trigger estate tax due when a person died: $650,000. For example:

If you passed away with a net worth of $650,000 or greater in 2001, which included your house and retirement accounts, your family would have paid estate tax, which had a maximum rate of 55 percent. Over the years, however, the value of estates subject to federal taxes has been raised by congress to $13,610,000 in 2024. In addition, the tax rate on estates over the federal tax limit now ranges from 18 to 40 percent. Some states, like my home state of Connecticut, also have a state estate tax, so that must be factored into your planning as well.

For those who have been fortunate and successful enough to have accumulated an estate valued at $13,610,000 or greater, I highly recommend estate planning from a tax perspective, in large part because there are strategies you can use to minimize potential estate taxes.

One final note on planning your estate: implementation is key. I've seen clients pay a lot of money for an estate plan, obtain the proper documents, and receive instructions for what to do, but never implement those instructions. In contrast, I've had clients complete their estate plan swiftly, and the assurance they feel afterward is immeasurable. I encourage you to be the latter. Your trusted fiduciary can help you achieve that same feeling of assurance, but only in partnership with you.

It is my sincere hope that you now feel educated and empowered to "Get It R-I-T-E" in planning for your future, and that you see a clear path forward in doing so.

Next, we're going to talk about Constructing Your Ultimate Portfolio, so that you can weigh the various risk and return options I typically recommend for my clients, and consider which types feel the most aligned with you and your particular life circumstance.

6

CONSTRUCTING THE ULTIMATE PORTFOLIO:

Choosing Investment Strategies Aligned with Your Life Plan

———

You are an individual with specific assets, needs, desires, and interests—and your investment strategies will, in large part, be a reflection of those things. As such, I am not attempting in this chapter to address the ideal investment scenario for every individual, nor am I suggesting a one-size-fits-all plan for everyone. What I will provide you with are easy-to-digest definitions of various assets and strategies, their advantages and disadvantages, and the reasons you may want to choose a particular one. I will also provide you with the five fundamental steps to help you build a strong foundation for your investment journey, as well as valuable tools and examples to make informed decisions. In short, this chapter is intended to give new and seasoned investors alike a simple reference guide for what investments can be comprised of, and why you might want to choose a specific strategy to your benefit.

Note here that while cryptocurrency is a viable and potentially lucrative—as well as risky—investment medium, it is not within my wheelhouse of expertise, and I therefore leave that topic to the experts who focus all of their attention on that market. Do keep in mind, however, as in following any investment guidance offered by the media, podcasts, newsletters, and the like, that charlatans and uninformed individuals abound. Do your research to be as confident as possible that you're taking advice in the crypto arena from someone you can trust.

DETERMINING YOUR INVESTMENT GOALS

As we discussed in the prior chapter in planning for retirement, it is vital to determine what your goals are before attempting to create a plan. The same is true before constructing your portfolio. Essentially, you want to identify the expenses or financial goals you have for the next five years, as well as those that extend beyond that time frame, to help you determine what funds you should allocate to each goal. If you have already done your retirement planning, some of those goals may come into play here, such as:

+ Being debt-free
+ Saving up a certain sum of money for a large purchase, such as a wedding
+ Buying a second home
+ Paying for your grandchildren's education or other pursuits of interest
+ Being able to travel or take vacations each year

If you have no specific goals within the next five years, it may be wise to focus on building your emergency fund (see page 126) and investing the rest of your money for the long term.

With regard to your investment strategies, you may have goals such as these:

+ Managing short- and long-term cash-flow needs
+ Consolidating investment accounts to make your investments easier to manage
+ Learning to better manage your investment portfolio
+ Building a low-cost investment portfolio to keep more of your money
+ Maximizing the return of your portfolio
+ Taking an occasional leap with high-risk investments in the hope of gaining high returns
+ Delegating the management of your investment portfolio to a professional so you can focus on other things

Again, becoming clear on your goals is the critical first step. Then, taking all of your wishes into account, and knowing what you're striving to achieve in both short- and long-term goals, your financial advisor can guide you on the various types and risk levels of investment strategies available to you.

Before we get into what these strategies look like, let's begin by breaking down the different asset classes you can choose to invest your money into so you can consider the risk versus reward tradeoff. The six asset classes you can invest in are: stocks (equities), bonds (fixed income), real estate (real estate investment trusts), commodities, cash, and private equity. We will cover each of these except for private equity, as this asset class is not readily accessible to most investors. We will also discuss the importance of having an emergency fund.

INVESTMENT STRATEGIES

Stocks

What Are They?

A stock is a security that represents the ownership of a segment of the issuing corporation. Units of stock are called "shares," which entitles the owner to a proportion of the corporation's assets and profits equal to how much stock they own.

Once a company issues shares, they can make them publicly or privately traded. Privately held stock is generally only accessible to owners and employers of that company. It is also extremely illiquid, as it can only be sold back to the company or to another investor as part of a merger or takeover. For this reason, we will focus on publicly traded stock, which is accessible to any investor.

Advantages

- ✦ Capital appreciation
- ✦ Voting rights
- ✦ Liquidity
- ✦ Potential dividends
- ✦ Hedge against inflation

Disadvantages

- ✦ Volatility
- ✦ Loss of principal

Why You Might Want to Invest in Stocks

If your goal is to maximize your returns over the long term, in real terms (net of inflation and taxes), you would want to invest the majority of your portfolio in stocks. Over long-term periods (ten years or greater), stocks have historically offered the most robust return of all the asset classes you can choose from. For example, stocks have a positive return 94 percent of the time over a ten-year period; over more than ten years, stocks have positive return 100 percent of the time. The chart below shows the range of returns for the S&P 500® based on the time period of being invested and the periods of negative returns.

S&P 500 INDEX HISTORICAL RISK & RETURN

1926–2022 Annualized Total Returns*			
Time Period	Range of Annualized Returns	Spread	Periods of Negative Returns
1 Year	-43.3% to 54%	97.3%	26.8%
2 Years	-34.8% to 41.7%	76.5%	16.7%
3 Years	-27% to 31.2%	58.2%	15.8%
5 Years	-12.5% to 28.6%	41.1%	12.9%
10 Years	-1.4% to 20.1%	21.5%	4.6%
15 Years	0.6% to 18.9%	18.3%	0.0%
20 Years	3.1% to 17.9%	14.8%	0.0%
25 Years	5.9% to 17.2%	11.3%	0.0%
30 Years	8.5% to 13.7%	5.2%	0.0%
35 Years	8.7% to 13.1%	4.4%	0.0%
40 Years	8.9% to 12.5%	3.6%	0.0%

*Source: S&P Dow Jones Indices
Past performance does not guarantee future results.

Bonds

What Are They?

Bonds are investment securities where an investor lends money to a company or government for a set period of time, in exchange for regular interest payments. Once the bond reaches maturity, the bond issuer returns the investor's money.

Advantages

+ Predictable income
+ Safety of principal (for investment grade or greater bonds)

Disadvantages

+ Not a good hedge against inflation, as bonds consistently earn less than inflation
+ Potential loss of principal due to bond defaults or early redemption losses (though these are generally less than stock losses)

Why You Might Want to Invest in Bonds

For investors with shorter-term goals who may not want the risk of owning stocks, real estate, or commodities, bonds can be an excellent means to have your money earn more than by merely leaving it in your bank account—especially if you are risk averse. Also, for retirees and pre-retirees, it can be advisable to leave a portion of your portfolio in bonds to protect against needing to withdraw from stocks, real estate, or commodities when those investments may be down in value.

Real Estate Investment Trusts

What Are They?

REITs, or real estate investment trusts, are companies that own or finance income-producing real estate across a range of property sectors. After meeting a number of requirements to qualify as REITs, they invest in entities such as offices, apartment buildings, warehouses, retail centers, medical facilities, data centers, telecommunications towers, infrastructure, and hotels. While REITs are both publicly traded and privately held, I advise investing in public only, as they have already been fully vetted by the public markets. Public REITs also offer greater liquidity, since they can be sold at any time and their price reflects their current market value.

Advantages

+ Good hedge against inflation (long-term returns)
+ Can generate passive income
+ Offer similar liquidity as stocks
+ Access to commercial real estate

Disadvantages

+ Can be as volatile as stocks
+ Passive income is not guaranteed and can fluctuate
+ Interest rate sensitive (changes in interest rates can negatively impact income and valuations)
+ Illiquid (private REITs may have lockup periods, and you may not be allowed to sell them when you want to)

Why You Might Want to Invest in Real Estate Investment Trusts

If you're interested in earning income from your portfolio with capital appreciation potential, or in diversifying your portfolio beyond stocks alone, REITs can be an option worth considering. You can own a single REIT that invests in one or a small number of properties, or through a mutual fund or exchange traded fund (ETF) that invests in multiple properties or sectors of the REIT markets.

Commodities

What Are They?

Commodities are raw materials used to manufacture consumer products, as well as basic staples, such as certain agricultural products. Commodities may include but are not limited to: oil, grains, ore, and natural gas.

Advantages

- ✦ Can generate short-term profits
- ✦ Can be a hedge against inflation
- ✦ Can offer diversification of your portfolio

Disadvantages

- ✦ Extreme volatility
- ✦ Long periods of declining prices
- ✦ Holding physical commodities can incur storage fees
- ✦ Commodities don't generate income for investors

Why You Might Want to Invest in Commodities

If you're seeking maximum diversification in your portfolio, adding commodities is a viable option. You can choose to add a single commodity like gold or silver, or gain broad exposure to the entire commodities sector through a mutual fund or exchange traded fund (ETF). This is especially true if you're investing in a retirement account, as it alleviates much of the difficulties of trading and storing physical commodities.

If you're interested in speculating or trading commodities, you can open a commodities future trading account (most commodities trade through what are known as futures contracts). I do caution you, however, as this can be a highly volatile and speculative investment.

Cash (or Cash Reserves)

What Is It?

As you would expect, cash (or cash reserves) is simply money you are keeping in cash, not in investments like stocks, bonds, REITs, or commodities, in the form of physical currency (bills or coins). You can keep this money inside of your brokerage account or in your bank account. Money market accounts or money market mutual funds also fall into this category.

Advantages

+ Liquidity, available immediately without any restrictions
+ No volatility (it won't fluctuate in value due to interest rate or stock market changes)

Disadvantages

✦ Terrible inflation hedge, as the cost of goods and services are constantly going up, meaning cash is losing its purchasing power on a daily basis

✦ Poor long-term investment (stocks, bonds, REITs, and commodities have returns that have outpaced cash over the long term)

Why Might You Want to Hold Cash?

It is always a good idea to have some cash on hand, simply because you never know when you might have an unexpected expense or emergency you need to cover. As such, you will want to keep a sum of money uninvested so that it will be readily available to you.

Why Money Market Funds or Money Market Mutual Funds Are the Best Place for Your Cash

Banks are notorious for offering very little benefit to their customers other than free checking and bill pay, and for paying negligible interest—often pennies on the dollar and well below the prevailing interest rate—on checking and savings deposits. For this reason, you should leave as little in your checking and savings accounts as possible.

What I recommend instead is to keep your cash in a money market account or money market mutual fund. These accounts will pay interest based on prevailing interest rates; over time, you will earn much more interest than leaving your money in the bank (or under your mattress!). As of the writing of this book—though dependent on current interest rates and subject to our

Federal Reserve—money markets are paying roughly 5 percent annual interest.

Money Market Funds

Also known as high-yield savings accounts, money market accounts are generally available through online banks. The interest rate they pay is adjustable due to changes from the Federal Reserve: if it lowers interest rates, the money market rate will decline; if it raises interest rates, the money market rate will increase.

A wonderful advantage of money market accounts is that you can link them to your bank account, with the option of transferring money from one to the other as needed. Although it requires an extra step to set up your accounts this way, you will earn more interest than your bank alone would pay, and some offer FDIC insurance if they are offered through a bank. For more information, you can check out www.bankrate.com or www.nerdwallet.com.

Money Market Mutual Funds

These differ from money market funds in that they are offered through mutual fund companies. Hundreds of these funds are available, mostly in short-term US government treasury securities. Though they don't offer FDIC insurance, these funds are considered one of the safest investments available. Do be advised, however, that some pay very little interest, akin to your bank, so be sure to do your own research and due diligence, or better yet, enlist the help of your financial advisor.

If your desire is to keep your money in one place, you may want to open a brokerage account where you have your retirement account. For example, the three largest brokerage firms in the United States are Charles Schwab, Fidelity, and Vanguard. All three offer money market mutual funds that pay high interest rates. I personally utilize both Charles Schwab and Fidelity for money market mutual funds. Some of these brokerage accounts also offer debit cards, check writing, and bill pay linked to the brokerage account—which means you may have access to features normally only available through your bank. This enables you to keep more money in your money market mutual fund and less in your bank account, allowing you to maximize the interest you earn on your cash.

Emergency Fund

What Is It?

An emergency fund typically holds three to six months' worth of living expenses in a liquid account, such as short-term CDs, short-term US Treasury bonds, money market funds, or cash. If you are still working and have a career with high turnover or income fluctuations, such as a sales position, or you are a business owner, you may want to consider increasing your emergency fund to hold one year of living expenses. I wouldn't, however, go beyond that, as you can be costing yourself long-term growth on those funds.

Advantages

This fund acts as a safety net in case of unexpected expenses, income reduction or fluctuation, or job loss. For example:

> If you suddenly needed $30,000 for a major expense, and all your money was invested in long-term stock funds, you would have to sell some of your stock to obtain the cash. If the stock market happened to be down in value at that time, you would risk losing money by selling at an untimely moment. This stock sale might also trigger unnecessary income tax. This is why having an emergency fund with readily available cash is crucial. It gives you the flexibility to wait and see if the stock market rebounds before selling your investments—and gives you better control of your income taxes.

Disadvantages

There are virtually no disadvantages to having this fund—except for having more than you need in it (such as more than a year's expenses, as mentioned above), or keeping it in a standard low-yield bank account. In this case, more of your money would grow at a low return or miss out on earning interest from a high-yield savings account or money market mutual fund.

ASSET ALLOCATION

Now that you have a sense of the different types of assets, let's look at asset allocation. While there are some general rules for this, the two primary factors to take into account are your specific financial goals and your comfort level with risk. We'll examine this in relation to retirement, as that is the most common reason to create an effective asset allocation plan.

We've discussed financial goals at length in this book already, so for this chapter, I want you to simply keep in mind that when you retire, you will rely on the income from your investment portfolio to achieve those goals you've set for yourself. As such, you will want to protect your nest egg by diversifying your assets to reduce the risk of significant declines in one particular investment. Your financial advisor will help to ensure that your investments align with your asset allocation and that you agree with the strategy he or she suggests for you.

One basic strategy is to subtract your age from 100 to determine the amount of money you should have in stocks. For example, if you are 60 years old and retiring, you should only have 40 percent in stocks. I believe this strategy, however, could be overly cautious. Another suggests subtracting your age from 120, which dictates that at 60 or 65, you should have 55 or 60 percent in stocks, respectively. While this is useful, I recommend looking at your strategy in a less general and more individualized way.

To guide your asset allocation decisions, you and your financial advisor should analyze sample portfolios to see how they've performed, then make decisions based on how much money you'll need from *your* portfolio. This is where you'll look closely at diversification, as well as your comfort with risk. (If, for example, you can't tolerate a 25 percent drop in your portfolio, even if a specific asset allocation could provide a higher return, it might not be appropriate for you.)

See the following page for hypothetical portfolio allocations.

Hypothetical Portfolio Allocations

	Fixed	Defensive	Conservative	Moderate	Aggressive	Equity
Equity / Stocks	0.0%	20.0%	40.0%	60.0%	80.0%	100.0%
US Stocks	0.0%	16.0%	32.0%	48.0%	64.0%	80.0%
Large-Cap Blend	0.0%	8.0%	16.0%	24.0%	32.0%	40.0%
Mid-Cap Blend	0.0%	3.0%	6.0%	9.0%	12.0%	15.0%
Small-Cap Blend	0.0%	3.0%	6.0%	9.0%	12.0%	15.0%
US Real Estate	0.0%	2.0%	4.0%	6.0%	8.0%	10.0%
Non-US Stocks	0.0%	4.0%	8.0%	12.0%	16.0%	20.0%
International	0.0%	3.0%	6.0%	9.0%	12.0%	15.0%
Emerging Markets	0.0%	1.0%	2.0%	3.0%	4.0%	5.0%
Fixed Income / Bonds	100.0%	80.0%	60.0%	40.0%	20.0%	0.0%
Intermediate Term	80.0%	60.0%	40.0%	20.0%	10.0%	0.0%
Short Term	20.0%	20.0%	20.0%	20.0%	10.0%	0.0%

For illustrative purposes only. Past performance is no guarantee of future results. The hypothetical portfolios are not recommendations for an actual allocation.

On the next page, you'll find examples of ETFs to give you an idea of what you could invest your portfolio in, many of which I use for my clients. Depending on where you keep your money, there may be other ETFs or index mutual funds that are appropriate for you.

Passive and Low-Cost ETFs

Investment Category	ETF Funds	Symbol	Annual Expense Ratio
Large-Cap Stock Index	SPDR® Portfolio S&P 500® ETF	SPLG	0.02%
Mid-Cap Stock Index	SPDR® Portfolio S&P 400™ Mid Cap ETF	SPMD	0.03%
Small-Cap Stock Index	SPDR® Portfolio S&P 600™ Small Cap ETF	SPSM	0.03%
US Real Estate Index	The Real Estate Select Sector SPDR® Fund	XLRE	0.09%
International Stock Index	SPDR® Portfolio Developed World ex-US ETF	SPDW	0.03%
Emerging Market Stock Index	SPDR® Portfolio Emerging Markets ETF	SPEM	0.07%
Intermediate-Term Bond Index	SPDR® Portfolio Aggregate Bond ETF	SPAB	0.03%
Short-Term Bond Fund	JP Morgan Ultra-Short Income ETF	JPST	0.18%
Short-Term Treasury Bond	SPDR® Bloomberg 3-12 Month T-Bill ETF	BILS	0.14%

This is not a recommendation to purchase a security. Past performance is no guarantee of future results. Investing in ETFs carries the risk of potential loss.

It is often said that "diversification is the only free lunch" in investing because, for the most part, diversifying your portfolio does not cost more than not doing so. In fact, we are currently at a point where investment costs have become so low that, in a well-diversified portfolio, you can drive fees to nearly zero without additional expenses.

Diversification can also help you stick to your plan when things get tough, as selling at the bottom is the worst thing you can do. Over twenty years of experience has taught me that when clients call me ready to abandon their plan during a market downturn, it's my job to help them stay invested; if I can prevent them from selling at the bottom, I've benefitted them tremendously.

Remember: it's time *in* the market not *timing the market*. In other words, if you're jumping in and out of the stock market to try to time the highs and lows, you are more likely to miss out on the gains than protect against losses. For example, if you missed only ten of the best days in the market over a 20-year period, beginning 1–1–2000 and ending 12–23–2019, you would have reduced your average annual return by over 50 percent, as shown in the following chart:

IMPACT OF BEING OUT OF THE MARKET

Returns of the S&P 500® Total Return Index
Performance of a $10,000 investment between
January 3, 2000 and December 31, 2019

Six of the best 10 days occurred within two
weeks of the 10 worst days

* The best day of 2015 (August 26) was only 2
days after the worst day (August 24)

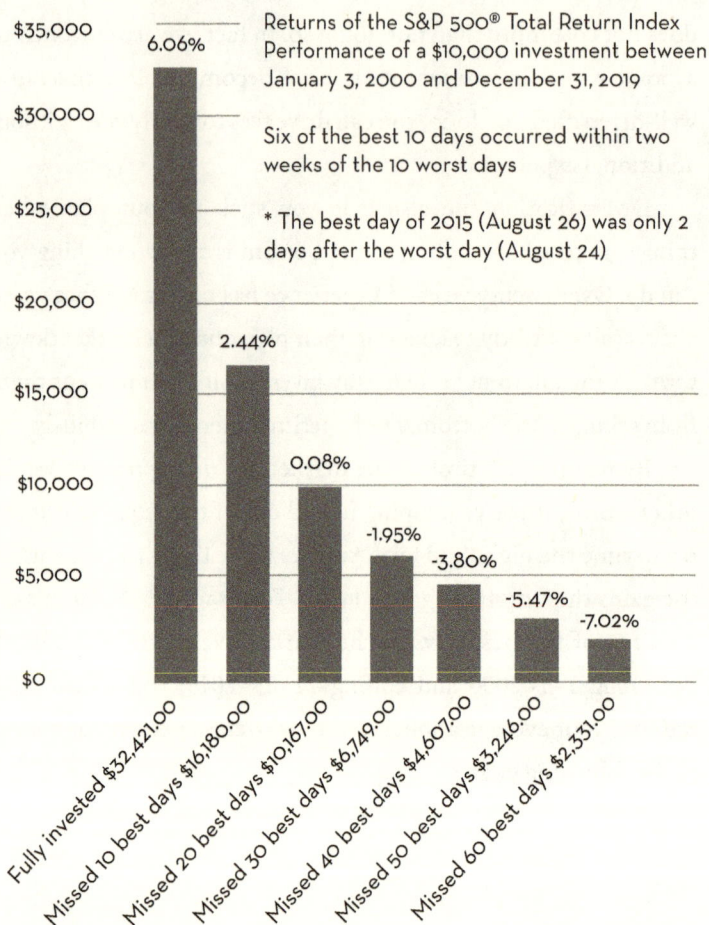

Returns are based on the S&P 500® Total Return Index. Indices do not include
fees or operating expenses and are not available for actual investment. Past
performance is not indicative of future returns.

The truth is, many people feel similar fear during a downturn and want to bail out of their investments altogether. When enough people act on those fears and sell, eventually the buying curve returns. In short, if you can weather the storm, you will almost always be better off in the long run.

During the COVID-19 pandemic, which marked the most recent and prolonged market decline, a lot of investors, including many of my clients, experienced fear and uncertainty about the future of their portfolios. A lot of my time was spent on the phone talking to clients about their investment plans and asset allocations. My role was to reassure them of their long-term plan and encourage them to remain committed, emphasizing that they had ample cash and bond holdings to weather the storm.

Many of my clients didn't need their money immediately, and I reminded them of this when they wanted to sell. Further, we had allocated 30 to 40 percent of their portfolio to safe investments like cash and bonds, neither of which were going anywhere. As a result, they had enough money in their conservative bucket to withstand a long decline, and most of my clients realized they would be okay even if the downturn lasted for a while. They could still pay their bills, remain retired, and avoid having to find a job to get by.

Asset allocation played a significant role in my clients being comfortable sticking with their portfolio, and that's my desire for you as well. Having a trusted fiduciary to counsel you can add tremendous value to your decision-making process. During a cultural or economic panic, you'll be much less likely to let the panic get to you and to make impulsive decisions. With a well-structured portfolio in place, you'll be confident in staying put and weathering the storm.

As a last note, to ensure clarity and consistency with clients, I use an **investment policy statement**—a simple two-page document that outlines not only the asset allocation within their portfolio, but also their life stage, income, list of assets, short- and long-term goals, and retirement goals. It also provides best and worst-case scenarios, which we review annually and update as needed.

I recommend you have this in writing from your financial advisor as well. It makes for an easy reference, and from a legal standpoint, it protects both you and your advisor. It's also useful if a successor advisor (or you, at some point) takes over your portfolio in the future. Overall, it is a good business practice on both sides to have documentation with regard to your investment plan. It reminds clients of the best- and worst-case scenario with their portfolio.

Now that we've talked about assets and their allocation, we'll take a brief look at the four types of investment strategies— active, passive, short-term, and long-term—so that you can evaluate which ones will be aligned with helping you accomplish your specific goals, at varying stages of your life.

Active Investment Strategy

What Is It?

An active investment strategy involves selecting specific securities you believe will do better than the market averages. For stocks, the market average is often measured by the S&P 500— the most popular US stock market index, which tracks the performance of the 500 largest companies in the United States. For example:

> If you selected 30 stocks from the S&P 500 to own for a year, you could then compare their performance to that of the index as a whole. If your 30-stock portfolio earned more than the S&P 500 index, you did your job and beat the market, so to speak. On the other hand, if your 30-stock portfolio earned less than the S&P 500, the market beat you. This is the goal of active investing: to beat the market averages over time. While it may sound easy, it is actually anything but.

Advantages

If, out of your 30 chosen stocks from the S&P, two of them happened to be top performers for the next ten years, your returns would be impressive and you may actually beat the market. However, keep in mind that studies have revealed a significant portion of success in active management is due to luck; the chances of selecting the best one or two stocks for the next ten years are extremely low. It's like hitting a winning lottery ticket.

Disadvantages

+ Statistically, **it is highly difficult to beat the market.** Even professionals fail to do it; studies show over long periods of time that it is not unusual to find only 20 percent of active asset managers have beaten their benchmark within a certain asset class, meaning 80 percent of mutual funds managed by professionals did not perform as well as their benchmark. If professionals who are trained and paid to do this job struggle to outperform their benchmark, the odds are definitely stacked against you as a solo investor. Much of Wall Street is set up to convince you that you and/or they can beat the market—and charge you high fees in the process.

✦ Engaging in daily trading activity means **you are vulnerable to making a wrong move**—such as selling just before the stock market goes up, or buying just before a price drop—as well as unnecessarily paying trading costs you could be saving and adding to your long-term return. Overall, the stock market has a lot of volatility, and my clients who have had the most investing success are the ones who don't attempt to time the highs and lows of the markets.

✦ Active management not only **incurs higher costs,** but also **increases the likelihood of failure** when attempting to pick winning stocks or other investments.

Why You Might Want to Invest in an Active Investment Strategy

To be honest, though I know some people like the excitement of risks that have the potential for big payoffs, I don't recommend investing in active strategies for the majority of your portfolio. It's okay to have a small portion invested in active investing, but the majority should be in passive strategies. The odds are not in your favor with active management, making it more akin to gambling than a strategic long-term investment approach.

Passive Investment Strategy

What Is It?

A passive investment strategy is the opposite of active investing. It involves owing a simple fund (often known as an index fund), like the S&P 500, based on the belief that the markets are efficient and can't be beaten over the long term. In other words, rather than try to beat the markets, you own the whole market. If it's stocks, no matter which stocks do the best, you own a piece of all of them. This means you follow the stock market in both good and bad times. This is how you capture all of the stock market's positive returns, which should be your ultimate goal.

This passive investing, or indexed investing strategy, can be done for your entire portfolio, meaning you can invest in index stock funds, index bond funds, index real estate funds, and index commodities funds. This is what I advocate for my clients and for my own money.

Advantages

Index funds consistently offer better returns than active funds, making them a more reliable option. A 2018 study titled "Investment Strategies That Beat the Market: What Can We Squeeze from the Market?" confirmed this in terms of long-term success.

Disadvantages

Some might say that index funds have the disadvantage of underperforming active funds. And yes, this might happen from year to year, especially in a bull market. However, over the long term, study after study has confirmed that index funds beat the majority of actively managed funds. Even though a small percentage of active funds might beat index funds over the long term, the challenge is in picking which active funds will beat their respective indexes. Remember, past performance is no indicator of future results.

While I see no disadvantage to index funds as a whole, not all are created equal. Some are more expensive than others, some might not be transferable to other companies, and some use different methodology than others. This is why your financial advisor will be helpful in developing and designing your portfolio. (Again, see examples on page 130.)

Why You Might Want to Invest in a Passive Investment Strategy

+ Though I used to be a proponent of active investing (because I knew no better), I have found **higher and more consistent returns** for my clients since shifting their portfolios toward passive investing—and I firmly believe that this strategy will continue to benefit my clients in the long term.

+ By consistently saving your money and using a passive strategy, you are **likely to outperform** most people who try to beat the market but end up making the wrong decisions, such as jumping in and out of the market or using funds that consistently underperform the market.

✦ The average cost of an active stock fund is roughly 1 percent, while the average passive fund costs about a tenth of a percent. This translates to **savings of almost 1 percent annually** that directly impacts your bottom line. The difference between active and passive bonds is similar, with a half-a-percent variance.

Sample Asset Allocation Investment Performance

To show how a sample asset allocation might perform, I put together the chart on the following page, using a Vanguard S&P 500 index fund (for stocks) and a Vanguard total bond market fund (for bonds) to create different portfolios. I started this comparison just before the 2008–2009 financial crisis to demonstrate the worst-case scenario of each asset allocation. Hopefully we will never see a repeat of that financial crisis; however, it is still important to expect the best but be prepared for the worst.

The takeaway here is understanding what the risk versus reward tradeoff is in your portfolio. In other words, you want to be comfortable with the potential decline during bad times so that you don't panic and exit the market prematurely.

SAMPLE ASSET ALLOCATION PERFORMANCE FROM
1-1-2007 TO 12-31-2021

Allocation* Stocks/Bonds	Maximum Drawdown	Time to Recover	Average Annual
100% Stocks	-43.28%	-1400 days	10.64%
90% / 10%	-38.96%	-1050 days	10.15%
80% / 20%	-34.59%	-820 days	9.62%
70% / 30%	-30.17%	-765 days	9.05%
60% / 40%	-25.71%	-650 days	8.44%
50% / 50%	-21.19%	-545 days	7.79%
40% / 60%	-16.63%	-335 days	7.11%
30% / 70%	-12.02%	-255 days	6.39%
20% / 80%	-7.4%	-180 days	5.64%
10% / 90%	-4.68%	-120 days	4.86%
100% Bonds	-3.49%	-90 days	4.05%

* Bonds represented by Vanguard Total Bond Index (VBTLX); stocks represented by Vanguard S&P 500® Index (VFIAX) and annually rebalanced.

As mentioned earlier, we use an investment policy statement in my firm that details the risk level and worst-case scenario for each client. This ensures that everyone is on the same page and understands the potential risks and benefits of their investment strategy.

Additionally, do make sure your advisor discloses any hidden fees for the strategies you choose, and that you're able to withdraw your money without penalty when you need access to it.

For a more in-depth education on an active versus passive

approach, I highly recommend the book, *The Only Guide to a Winning Investment Strategy You'll Ever Need*, by Larry E Swedroe.

Short-Term Investments

What Are They?

Short-term investments encompass money you'll need access to within five years. Why five years? Because this is how long the average stock market cycle lasts. In other words, if you'll need your money in less than five years, there's a strong likelihood you can lose money during that time. For this reason, I would avoid the riskier asset classes of stocks, REITs, and commodities for short-term investments. Instead, I recommend investing in:

+ Short-term bonds
+ Short-term bond funds
+ CDs
+ Money market funds

Note that in the event you have goals that move from the long-term to short-term category, you will likely need to adjust your investment strategy, meaning pulling some funds from your long-term bucket and putting them into your short-term bucket.

Advantages

If you avoid the riskier asset classes, there should be little chance of principal loss, and you should be able to grow your money at a rate greater than leaving it in your bank account.

Disadvantages

+ Relying only on short-term investments to grow your wealth is typically not the best long-term strategy.

+ Short-term investments often barely keep pace with inflation. They don't grow your money in real terms, net of inflation and taxes.

+ For many investors, the constant fear of short-term loses in the stock, real estate, and commodities markets cause them to keep too much money in short-term investments, costing them valuable long-term gains.

Why You Might Want to Make Short-Term Investments

+ Saving for a house

+ Saving for a child's college education that will commence within a few years

+ Saving for a near-term wedding for yourself or one of your children

Long-Term Investments

What Are They?

Long-term investments, such as for retirement funds, typically encompass real estate, stocks, and commodities. Each of these investments provide growth opportunities that can outpace inflation rates.

Advantages

+ Good hedge against inflation
+ Potential to build significant wealth
+ Potential to leave a significant inheritance

Disadvantages

+ Potential short-term losses
+ Potential long-term periods of lower-than-expected gains

Why You Might Want to Make Long-Term Investments

+ If your aim is to grow your money in real terms, after inflation and taxes, you must have a long-term perspective. Focusing on anything else will not be beneficial.

+ You're saving for a child's college education that won't commence for five or more years, in which case it would be appropriate to consider a more diversified portfolio, including high-risk investments, to provide potential growth to help offset the cost of education.

+ You're saving for your retirement and/or living off your funds during your retirement.

THE FIVE STEPS TO INVESTMENT PLANNING

I've amassed a great deal of knowledge about investing through experience and training, as well as from many books—and one of the best books I've read is *The Investment Answer* by Daniel C. Goldie and Gordon S. Murray (2011). In it, the authors lay out investing in a five-step process I find useful, especially for new investors working with a financial advisor. I will share the steps here in condensed form, but I highly recommend the book for the expanded education you'll receive from it.

Step 1: Determine Your Asset Allocation

When I meet with prospective clients who already have a portfolio, few of them know what their asset allocation is. Whether they're managing their own investments, or—even scarier—they have a financial advisor, they often have no idea what the risk level is in their portfolio. Either they're not aware of risks they're taking, or their advisor isn't keeping them informed about what he or she is doing for them. The bottom line is: your asset allocation is the core tenet of investing. The good news is, it's an easy element to control.

Ask yourself:

+ What risk level am I comfortable with?

+ Are my investment products the right mix for me?

+ Can I stay with this allocation through both good and bad markets?

+ Are my investments generating a lot of unnecessary taxes?

Then, look at the actual investment products you're in and ask:

Would I be better served in other products that have lower fees and possibly better results?

Most people agree that the closer you get to retirement, the more conservative you'll want to be. This is because you don't have as much time to endure a market recovery. In recent years, for example, investments have gone down 30 to 40 percent in value—some of the worst market declines we've seen. This is why I recommend protecting some of your portfolio by allocating more to bonds and cash than to stocks (the closer you get to retirement)—and not winging it when it comes to your investing.

Step 2: Decide How Diversified You Want to Be

In simplest terms, this step asks you to consider how diversified a portfolio you want to have. There are no rules here: if you want maximum diversification, you can include all five asset classes; if you want to keep it simpler, you can. Questions to ask yourself are:

✦ Do I want to have a standard portfolio of stocks, bonds, and cash?

✦ Do I want to include REITs and commodities?

✦ Within stocks, how many segments of the market do I want to own? Do I want to own large-cap stocks only, or medium- and small-cap stocks too?

✦ Will I want to include international stocks?

✦ Will I want to include emerging markets stocks?

I've included these questions because I find that most investors think very little about diversification. Many are accidental investors, buying what a friend recommends or taking advice from an article in a financial magazine, rather than having a specific investment plan. But weighing which assets you want to invest in is an important part of developing your portfolio and investment policy statement. Yet another benefit of your fiduciary partnership is that he or she can help you with these decisions if you are unsure.

Step 3: Decide If You Want to Be an Active or a Passive Investor

As I explained earlier, this is the difference between predicting and choosing which stocks, commodities, or real estate sectors will be the best investment (active) versus investing broadly across multiple markets (passive). While this is your decision, a multitude of studies support the latter type of investing, and this is what I always recommend.

Step 4: Rebalancing Asset Allocation

Once you solidify your plan, and your asset allocation is set, you and your financial advisor must manage it, meaning having a strategy for managing your portfolio through the ups and downs of the markets as well as withdrawals from your portfolio. For example:

Let's say your target asset allocation is 60 percent stock funds and 40 percent bond funds. Then the stock market goes down, making your portfolio 50 percent stock funds and 50 percent bond funds. Do you leave it alone? Or do you buy more stock funds to get your portfolio back in line with your target allocation? Although buying when things are down may seem counterintuitive, it's better to sell some bonds and buy stocks because stocks are currently more affordable. If you don't have a strategy in place, you're more likely to let emotion dictate your rebalancing strategy.

The important takeaway here is that once you set up an overall strategy for your investments, you, along with your financial advisor, will need to monitor it on a quarterly, semiannual, or annual basis. You will also want to determine if certain triggering events—taking your allocation out of alignment by, say, 5 percent—will be cause for rebalancing.

Step 5: Do It Yourself or Hire a Professional

In *The Investment Answer*, the authors discuss managing your own portfolio versus hiring a professional to help you. As *Fiduciary* is focused on finding, hiring, and establishing an aligned and trusted partnership with a fee-only financial advisor, we won't talk here about managing your own portfolio. But if you do decide to dabble in some investments on your own, the above steps will hopefully help you chart a beneficial path.

In summary, the simpler you keep your investment strategy, the better off you'll be in constructing your ultimate portfolio. When you believe you're smarter than the market, or smarter than the professionals, you'll most likely do yourself a disservice. Instead, I recommend developing a predominately index-based portfolio. If you want to own some individual stocks, it's certainly okay to have a little fun with your money—but I recommend keeping it less than 10 percent of your total portfolio. Yes, it's important to follow the markets. But in my experience, using a diversified index-based strategy is more advantageous than striving to beat the markets, where fluctuations are largely unpredictable and impossible to hit just right on a regular basis.

I also recommend taking the long view on the majority of your investments. Research shows that this visionary perspective is beneficial for achieving sustainable success. By focusing on building a diverse portfolio, embracing a long-term outlook, and staying the course, you as an investor will have an excellent chance of weathering short-term market fluctuations and achieving your financial goals over the long haul.

In the next chapter, we'll look specifically at what types of strategies to avoid when considering investments. While your fiduciary should never try to steer you into these, I want to be sure you're aware of them so that your portfolio remains productive for you, and that you don't get taken in the event you decide to experiment with investing on your own.

7

STAYING IN THE EARNING ZONE:

Steering Clear of Losing Strategies

———◇———

When it comes to investing, as in most things, if something sounds too good to be true, it usually is. Scams may be repackaged to look appealing, but they are still scams—and unfortunately, gimmick investment products abound. This is why I adhere to strict investment philosophies and steer clear of certain products that may put my clients' money at risk, and why you should expect the same of your financial advisor. To that end, this chapter will focus on some of the most commonly promoted investment products and schemes I advise you to avoid, in the hope you'll never be taken by the empty promises they offer.

As in the previous chapter, I will define each one for clarity. Unlike the previous chapter, however, I will share multiple examples of how and why these are detrimental, so that you understand the ways they can be misrepresented as a potential benefit to you, and so that you'll be able to identify the red flags.

STRATEGIES TO AVOID

Variable Annuities

What Are They?

A variable annuity is a contract between you and an insurance company that serves as an investment account. This account:

+ may grow on a tax-deferred basis

+ includes certain insurance features, such as the ability to turn your account into a stream of periodic payments

+ is purchased either via a single purchase payment or a series of purchase payments

+ offers a range of investment options

+ will vary in value depending on the performance of the investment options you choose

+ offers investment options, called sub-accounts (designed to mimic mutual funds), that invest in stocks, REITS, commodities, bonds, money market instruments, or some combination of these.

Drawbacks of Variable Annuities

The biggest drawback to investing in these annuities is the fees—and what's worse is that the fees are often not disclosed to you on an ongoing basis, nor are they easily understood. They are supposed to be presented and explained at the time of purchase, but more often they are buried in the fine print. Further, it's not common to receive an annual invoice that shows the amount of fees you paid over the last year, so unless you know where to dig to find this information, you'll be completely in the dark.

To complicate it further, there are three layers of fees with variable annuities: the mortality expense, the fund or sub-account costs, and what are called "rider fees." It's not crucial to understand each of these fees; all you need to know is that they can add up to 2.5 to 4 percent a year for investor expenses. While that number may seem low, the impact is extremely high.

Here is an example:

As I mentioned in the definition above, **stocks** and **bonds** are two of the investment options within a variable annuity. Your **stock** investment is based on what the future stock returns are going to be. Let's assume those future returns are going to be 8 percent for the next ten years. Only it's not actually 8 percent because unbeknownst to you, you're paying an extra 3.5 percent per year in annuity fees, reducing your return to 4.5 percent per year. If you're more conservative, and you choose to invest mostly in bonds inside these annuities, it could be even worse. With an expected bond return of 4.5 percent per year, with 3.5 percent per year in annuity fees, there's almost zero potential to earn any returns on your money over a long period of time. This is why high fees in annuities—especially variable annuities—are so detrimental to your portfolio.

Yet another drawback of variable annuities is the fact that they are often sold on commission—and the commission rates are high, which is part of the reason the ongoing fees are so high. You already know the conflict of interest involved when financial advisors sell commission-based products; this is why the guidance in this book is focused solely on engaging an authentic fee-only fiduciary, in part to ensure this conflict of interest won't exist in your partnership. However, you may currently be working with a broker and already invested in annuities, such as in the example that follows:

> I recently met with a prospective client who invested $500,000 into a variable annuity with his broker eleven years ago. Over that timeframe, we had an excellent run in the stock market, and he should have averaged about an 8 percent return per year. Instead, because of the fees he was paying and the poor investments he was put into by his broker, he made only 1 percent per year over the eleven years inside the variable annuity. The broker made his hefty upfront commission selling the client into this annuity, yet the client didn't grow his money at all, when it should have more than doubled during those eleven years. The annuities fees and poor investment options cost this client significantly.

In another example:

> A client I've been working with for years recently attended a dinner seminar where she was offered a "free review" of her existing portfolio by a so-called advisor. In that review, she was advised to invest all her retirement money in a high-cost variable annuity. Fortunately, my

client—who is already in a diversified low-cost index-based portfolio—sought my input before making any decisions. In reviewing the fees associated with the annuity, I highlighted the differences in cost between the new investment options and her existing strategy: the variable annuity would incur additional fees of 2.5 percent per year above her existing portfolio, reducing her potential future returns. The so-called advisor neglected to tell her about these additional fees, or about the hefty upfront commission he would receive by her making this change. Sadly, in recommending these expensive products, it seemed the advisor was only interested in making a profit (and, perhaps, recovering the money spent on an expensive dinner seminar). Luckily, I was able to prevent my client from making a disastrous decision.

These examples drive home how variable annuities frequently benefit the seller (advisor), not the buyer (client). Advisors who sell these products often look through rose-colored commission glasses without considering how the additional costs and poor investment options are going to impact a client's long-term success.

I'll be honest here: all advisors can make mistakes, particularly early in our careers, and especially if we don't know any better. I, myself, had clients who were interested in variable annuities, and I invested some of their money in one of these products, believing I was doing the right thing for them. What I ended up finding, however, was that over the five-year period they were in this variable annuity portfolio, it significantly lagged in market returns. The stock market had average gains during this time, but the funds they could choose from in their variable annuity performed very poorly. These limited volatility funds were designed to protect the client's downside losses, but they instead cost them upside gains. They had invested $100,000 into the variable annuity, which should have grown to $150,000 with a standard index fund within the investment period, but instead only grew to $104,000. As soon as I realized the dubiousness of this strategy, I had my clients exit the variable annuity, but the damage was already done. That was the end for me of using broker-sold variable annuities for clients.

Many annuities sold by brokers also carry what's known as a surrender charge, a penalty or fee you as a client will have to pay to withdraw your money from the annuity. These surrender charges range in the length of time they apply, up to ten years, with penalties starting as high as 10 percent.

Here is an example of how a ten-year surrender schedule would work:

Year	%	Year	%
1	10%	6	5%
2	9%	7	4%
3	8%	8	3%
4	7%	9	2%
5	6%	10	1%
Year 11 = 0%			

Say you invest $100,000 into a variable annuity, and in the first year need your $100,000 back. You would pay a $10,000 (10 percent) penalty to get your money. These surrender charges can be extremely costly to you, especially within the first few years. This is another negative of investing your money into an annuity.

Unfortunately, I meet with prospective clients all the time who have been working with brokers and were sold variable annuities. When I review these products they're in and see how poor their performance has been, my heart drops. I've even had clients tell me they've questioned their advisor multiple times about why they were investing in a variable annuity, only to be continually told it was a great investment and that they were doing fine. It was only when they met with me and I identified what was actually happening within their portfolios that they had their feelings validated.

Overall, I see a lot of money that should be remaining in the pocket of everyday investors but is bleeding out through variable annuity fees.

Non-Traded Real Estate Investment Trusts (REITs)

What Are They?

A non-traded REIT, sometimes called a private REIT, is one that is not traded on major stock exchanges and as such is **illiquid**, meaning you generally cannot withdraw your money when you want to or sell your shares as with a public REIT. In other words, if you invested $10,000, and a year later you wanted your money back, you typically couldn't get it out. The REIT might allow for a small percentage of liquidations per year, such as 5 percent of the total REIT; otherwise, there must be a liquidation event to withdraw your money. In this case, the fund is sold to another fund, or it goes public, allowing you to sell your shares on the open market. Until a liquidation event happens, however, you have no control over your investment and your money remains locked up.

In contrast, a **liquid** REIT, or publicly traded REIT, is one that trades on a major stock market exchange, where you can sell any day the stock market is open, usually 255 days a year.

Drawbacks of (Illiquid) Non-Traded REITS

As stated above, the major drawback is that your money is locked into the REIT until it has a liquidation event—and the sale is not your decision to make.

Let's look at an example.

With a non-traded REIT, the money in the initial phase is raised for the private real estate fund. They set a target size for the fund—say, a billion dollars. As the money is raised, the managers of the REIT (the general partners) begin to buy up (invest) the money of the fund into commercial properties. They continue doing this until they invest all the money in the fund. The investors in the fund (you) are called limited partners, while the general partners call all the shots.

The REIT will usually have a target annual distribution rate, or dividend. Let's say it is 7 percent, meaning that the goal of the REIT will be to pay investors 7 percent per year, net the operating fees from the rents they collect on the properties. They also hope to grow the value of the fund, or at least keep the value stable, by buying quality commercial properties that will appreciate, or at minimum hold their value. One of the initial problems these funds have is that until the fund is fully invested and generating cash flow, the managers may be obligated to pay the 7 percent dividend to the investors— which can hurt the fund's long-term performance.

I've had some experience with these non-traded REITs. The initial one I invested clients into did fine. They received their 7 percent dividends, and about eighteen months after the clients made their initial investment, there was a liquidation event, whereby they were able to sell their shares for about 20 percent above what they bought them for. Many of these clients were delighted with this result, and we decided to invest in a few other non-traded REITs.

Unfortunately, these subsequent non-traded REITs didn't do nearly as well as the initial ones. Most paid their dividend for only a few years, eventually having to cut their dividends in half. This lower dividend reduced the value of the non-traded REIT anywhere from 30 to 70 percent of the clients' initial investment. Though all of us were aware that investing in REITs came with risk of loss, the devaluation was not what I or my clients expected.

To make matters worse, because this was an illiquid investment, my clients couldn't sell their shares when the value of the REIT began to decline, to prevent further losses and invest their money in something else. Many of these clients still own shares of these non-traded REITs and are waiting for a liquidation event to unload their shares.

Sadly, my story isn't unique when it comes to investing in non-traded REITs. There are myriad stories like mine over the last ten years alone, where the dividend was cut or eliminated, the value of the REIT plummeted, and the clients were left stuck in the REIT because there has been no liquidation event.

In my case, I believe it was a combination of bad timing, poor management by the general partners, and excessive fees that caused many of these non-traded REITs to have the problems they've had. Additionally, because they are non-traded, their price is only determined once a year by an independent auditor, in contrast to the 255 days per year with publicly traded REITs. This lack of transparency often leads to additional problems for investors, as any problems with the REIT can go undisclosed to investors for up to a year.

Before I knew better, I was told these non-traded REITs were a solid alternative for clients looking for income and pre-dictability in retirement. But as I have found, this has rarely been the case. Had I known the limitations ahead of time, I never would have recommended this strategy to my clients; instead, I would have steered them toward liquid, or publicly traded, REITs. Even though these would have offered a lower initial dividend, we would have been able to exit these funds if they experienced the problems of the non-traded REITs. Don't get me wrong: publicly traded REITs carry high risk and can be even more volatile than stocks at times. However, the added liquidity and ongoing price discovery is a major benefit over non-traded REITs.

As a final note, if you have interest in owning real estate pri-vately, I suggest buying your own individual properties, whereby you have control over the buying, selling, and management of your properties, rather than having a general partner control it as part of a fund.

Cash Value Life Insurance

What Is It?

Cash value life insurance is a policy that lasts for the lifetime of the holder and features a cash value savings component. The policyholder can use the cash value for various purposes, including borrowing or withdrawing cash from it, or using it to pay policy premiums. The policy is purchased for a certain amount, such as a $250,000 death benefit, and you deposit money toward that amount until it is reached. If you die prior to the total being reached, the insurance company is liable for the difference.

Drawbacks of Cash Value Life Insurance

The first glaring drawback is that cash value life insurance is sold by brokers, generally career agents who work for one of the major life insurance companies. You already know what this means: high commissions, with little regard for the disadvantages to the client.

Here is an example scenario:

> A client tells her agent she's looking to save more for retirement, with an extra $600 a month to put aside. Without offering options—such as investing into an index fund that will contribute to her retirement account, among others, with pros and cons of each—the agent sells her hard on cash value life insurance. It is no coincidence that the agent receives a substantial commission on this product: up to 70 percent of the first-year premium. In numbers:

A $600 a month premium equals $7,200 a year. The agent receives 70 percent of that total premium, which is a $5,040 commission, simply for selling the product to the client.

If instead the agent recommended a portfolio and charged her 1 percent per year to manage that portfolio, the agent would only receive $72 in fees (1 percent times $7,200).

So yes, the high commission is a red flag, but why is cash value life insurance not a good investment overall?

Essentially, most of the premium ($600 per month in our example) pays for the costs of the policy, while only part goes into your investment account within the policy. This account earns interest based on the performance of the index fund you and your agent choose in the policy. If the index goes up, you earn interest; if the index goes down, you don't. However, these high fees that pay for the cost of the policy, along with the substantial upfront commission the agent receives, take a long time to recover from—so long that it can take many years until the policy breaks even from what you invest into it. This is why investing in an index fund, or even a CD, is a better option than using cash value life insurance as a savings or investment account.

Your agent may hard-sell you on the perk of borrowing against or withdrawing from this type of policy if you need access to your funds. And it's true that if you borrow from the policy, the loan is tax-free. However, the IRS requires that you be charged interest on this loan by the insurance company, or it won't be tax-free. This interest can be substantial, ranging from 5 to 8 percent per year. What's more, cash value life insurance carries surrender charges that can last up to fifteen years, meaning if you want full access to your money, it would be subject to penalties for up to fifteen years.

In sum, if you run the numbers comparing cash value life insurance with an index fund, the index fund far and away exceeds the benefits of the cash value life insurance.

Though the focus of this chapter is strategies to avoid, in this section, I don't want to merely steer you away from cash value life insurance without giving you a more beneficial alternative. Hence, I will discuss here what I recommend instead.

Alternatives to Cash Value Life Insurance

Term Life Insurance

If you don't already have a term life insurance policy, you've likely heard of this type of insurance, perhaps wondering how it differs from the cash value option. I will lay that out for you here.

Let's say you decide you need half a million dollars of life insurance to ensure your family will be all right if you die prematurely. The least expensive way to do this is to buy term insurance, which means it covers you if you die during a specified term. The most common term insurance is for 20 years.

In simplest terms, you buy a 20-year policy, and if you die during those 20 years, your family receives half a million dollars. If you live beyond that, your family receives nothing because, presumably, you have lived to retirement age, your children are grown, and your spouse is supported by your retirement funds, Social Security survivor benefit, and possibly a pension.

This may seem like a huge risk to take for insurance you may never need, but for many, it offers peace of mind in the event they die unexpectedly. Think of it as similar to paying into auto insurance every year for 20 years and never having an accident. If you need them, the funds are there; if you don't, they are absorbed into the funds paid out to others. It's not a perfect system, no doubt, but that's the way insurance works.

Monthly payments for term insurance are based on your age, health when you apply, and the amount of insurance you buy. Let's examine what this might look like in numbers, in comparison to the cash value life insurance.

Let's say you're 45 and need $500,000 of additional life insurance. The monthly payment for the term life insurance you choose is $100, whereas the payment for the $500,000 cash value policy (from our example on page 159) is $600. The difference between the two is $500 a month. What would justify such a difference each month for a life insurance policy?

For **you**, the term insurance does have a risk: remember, if you live past the term (our example is 20 years), your policy is forfeited.

For **the agent**, the commission paid on the term insurance is much less: if you pay $1,200 per year in premiums ($100 per month) instead of $7,200 per year ($600 per month), and the agent earns 70 percent either way, he or she is looking at $840 in commission instead of $5,040. While a clear conflict of interest, that's a huge motivating element that's not in your favor as a client.

This leads to the third and perhaps biggest factor: the investment opportunity.

Instead of paying $100 for the term insurance, the agent may encourage you to pay the additional $500 for the cash value insurance, investing it into the insurance policy because it will be tax-free in retirement. Here's where people can be sold on an option that will grow their money—which sounds good—when in reality, there are much better options for doing that.

Case in point: Over the long term, if you compare how your additional $500 were to perform within a cash value policy versus you taking that $500 and investing it in an index fund like the S&P 500, you'd have much more money at the end of twenty years by investing in the S&P 500 than you would in the cash value life insurance.

This is the scam that's sold to people.

And this is why in my practice, we adhere to the philosophy of: "Buy term, invest the difference." In other words, you are better off buying term insurance and investing the difference in premium into an index fund.

Guaranteed Universal Life Insurance

A reputable advisor will tell you that if you want permanent life insurance, meaning it will pay your beneficiaries no matter when you die, you would want to purchase what is known as guaranteed universal life (GUL).

This is a type of permanent life insurance policy that offers lifelong protection with fixed premiums and a guaranteed death benefit. The policyholder can customize premium payments and payment schedules to their needs, within limits, and GUL does not build cash value. What this means is that you are paying for the purchase cost of life insurance, not investing money within the policy. What's more, the policyholder can choose the duration of coverage, which can range from 90 to 121 years (opting for a longer coverage length is advisable to ensure the policy does not expire before the policyholder does).

This GUL policy is best if you want to leave a certain amount of money to your beneficiaries and are worried about spending down your retirement funds. As with all life insurance, the death benefit is also tax-free to beneficiaries.

Pump and Dump

What Is It?

Pump and dump is a manipulative scheme that attempts to boost the price of a stock or security through fake recommendations. This is accomplished when a group buys a reasonable amount of shares (or coin, within the cryptocurrency space) in an entity that doesn't have a lot of activity or favorable news. The group then spreads the word about the entity having a product or innovation that will increase their earnings. This creates a buzz that drives the price up. People then buy into it based on this news and on observing the rising price. Once that occurs, the original group of buyers—essentially con artists—sell their shares (stock, coin) to make a profit, while those left holding these shares lose money once the deceitful buzz is either realized or stops spreading, whereby the price plummets.

Drawbacks and Signs of Pump and Dump

The definition alone should tell you that you want nothing to do with this kind of fraudulent scheme. The slim chance of making gains through deceiving others is never a path you want to take, and your advisor should certainly never engage in such a practice, nor should they encourage it.

So that you're aware of where these commonly appear, here are two examples.

The practice of pump and dump is most common with **penny stocks,** which have a low price, generally less than $5 but some for literal pennies. These stocks are often not traded on major stock exchanges, such as the Nasdaq or NYSE, making them more susceptible to fraud.

These fraudsters will buy up a large amount of a penny stock and launch the rumor mill that it's a winner, urging their friends and family to buy shares. Once the stock goes up enough, they dump their shares, leaving the people not in on the con with major losses. The movies *Boiler Room* and *The Wolf of Wall Street* are excellent examples of this.

The latest pump and dump scheme is "**meme stocks,**" where social media has made it easier than ever to spread false news about stocks, expressly for the purpose of drawing uninformed investors into buying shares (such as in the 2023 film *Dumb Money*). Certain Facebook groups have lured more people into investing, as well as a group within Reddit called Wall Street Bets, the focus of which is to stick it to Wall Street by buying stocks Wall Street didn't like or is betting against. As with penny stocks, if enough people buy these shares, they can force the stock to go up in value rather than down, thereby making money while bleeding Wall Street. If you jump in early with this meme stock craze, it's possible to make a lot of money; however, if you're a late adopter of a certain stock, you can lose a fortune. This is because eventually, people will sell their shares and take their profits, and you don't want to be one of the last to get out before that stock crashes.

This also occurs with crypto.

I'll occasionally see someone I vaguely know on Facebook talking about crypto coins, telling their followers how great they are and how they've made loads of money investing in them. Over time, I see this person promoting certain coins—or one specific coin—only to eventually find out that the coin crashed shortly after posting all their hype about it.

In either case, this kind of narrowly focused promotion typically stems from a small group of people who own a lot of particular shares or coins, then pump it up to get people to jump in, believing it's a great investment. Then, the majority group collectively sells without the "jumpers" having a clue, causing them to lose a great deal of their money, or even all of their money.

In sum, if you want to buy individual stocks or coins, make sure to do your own research, and that you fully understand what the company does, how they make money, and what their earnings outlook is. In short: don't get caught up in the mania.

Ponzi Schemes—or Worse

What Are They?

Ponzi schemes are named after Charles Ponzi, who duped investors in the 1920s with a postage stamp speculation scheme. It is essentially an investment fraud, headed by someone who promises you a specific fixed rate of return that's higher than you could achieve with a safe investment, paying existing investors with funds collected from new investors.

Ponzi scheme organizers often promise to invest your money and generate high returns with little or no risk, but in many Ponzi schemes, the fraudsters don't invest the money; instead, they use it to pay those who invested earlier and often keep some for themselves. With little or no legitimate earnings, Ponzi schemes require a constant flow of new money to survive. When it becomes hard to recruit new investors, or when large numbers of existing investors cash out, these schemes tend to collapse.

Drawbacks and Signs of Ponzi Schemes

As with the pump and dump, the definition alone should tell you that you want nothing to do with this fraudulent scheme. Some of these companies market themselves in a way that makes them look highly knowledgeable, transparent, and trustworthy, but rarely if ever live up to their advertising. The following signs, taken from the Investor.gov website, are excellent and will alert you to a potential Ponzi scheme:

+ **High returns with little or no risk.** Every investment carries some degree of risk, and investments yielding higher returns typically involve more risk. Be highly suspicious of any "guaranteed" investment opportunity.

+ **Overly consistent returns.** Investments tend to go up and down over time. Be skeptical about an investment that regularly generates positive returns regardless of overall market conditions.

+ **Unregistered investments.** Ponzi schemes typically involve investments that are not registered with the SEC or with state regulators. Registration is important because it provides investors with access to information about the company's management, products, services, and finances.

+ **Unlicensed sellers.** Federal and state securities laws require investment professionals and firms to be licensed or registered. Most Ponzi schemes involve unlicensed individuals or unregistered firms.

+ **Secretive, complex strategies.** Avoid investments if you don't understand them or can't get complete information about them.

+ **Issues with paperwork.** Account statement errors may be a sign that funds are not being invested as promised.

✦ **Difficulty receiving payments.** Be suspicious if you don't receive a payment or have difficulty cashing out. Ponzi scheme promoters sometimes try to prevent participants from cashing out by offering even higher returns for staying put.

To give a simple example:

A safe investment would be obtaining a one-year CD from your local bank. Let's say it offered a 2 percent return, but a friend of yours tells you he has a great investment strategy that will guarantee you 10 percent a year. So, you put your money into this investment "fund." It takes a while, but eventually people start asking for their money back. Because there's not enough money coming in to support the money going out, the whole thing blows up, revealing it was nothing more than a Ponzi scheme.

Here is an even worse example:

I grew up down the street from and graduated high school with a guy who became a financial advisor. I didn't stay in touch with him, but I heard he'd been in business for about fifteen years, had a lot of clients, and was doing well. Then the news broke that he had stolen money from a client.

This client was an elderly woman who was legally blind. She and this advisor had formed a friendly relationship, and she had added him as a joint tenant to her bank account, which had $600,000 in it, giving him unrestricted access. He was supposed to help this woman pay her bills and make withdrawals and deposits, but this louse ended up draining her entire bank account. Eventually, the theft was discovered and the authorities alerted, after which the so-called advisor was sentenced to over three years in jail.

I don't know for certain if they recovered any of this woman's money, but the advisor was barred forever from holding a job in the financial industry. He not only caused immense damage to his client, but also to the reputation and level of trust within the industry.

Case in point: Never add someone as a joint tenant on your bank account, unless you are certain they are trustworthy. As a joint tenant, they have full access to your money.

Another incident occurred recently in the crypto space:

A multitude of people believed they were lending money to the FTX cryptocurrency exchange at 12 percent interest, when at the time we could barely earn 1 percent interest within a US bank. This 12 percent interest promise turned out to be a Ponzi scheme. Although it sounded too good to be true, most people didn't take the steps to critically analyze what they were investing in.

The final example I'll leave you with isn't technically a Ponzi scheme but, depending on the investment and outcome, can be even worse: investing in a "limited partnership." While I won't delve into the complexities of the various types of limited partnerships in this book, suffice it to say it is an investment strategy I don't recommend and that you should probably avoid.

Jeff, a police officer client I helped long ago with retirement planning, had met an advisor (before seeking my help) who told him he was a former Army veteran who liked helping people in the armed forces. Jeff appreciated this and accepted when the advisor invited Jeff to a fancy dinner at Ruth's Chris Steakhouse. At the end of the meal, which included an investment pitch, Jeff decided to invest some money with the advisor in a limited partnership related to diamond mines.

When Jeff told me in a meeting about this investment, I was concerned and asked to see his statement. When he told me he didn't receive a statement, my concern grew stronger. "How do you know what your investments are worth?" I asked.

"The advisor comes to our house periodically and writes the value on a piece of paper," he said.

I couldn't believe what I was hearing and told him he needed to get a legitimate statement immediately.

After pushing for months for this statement, Jeff finally learned that the diamond mine hadn't panned out and that his investment was worth nothing. I then advised him to contact the authorities and file a police report. It was no surprise when I did more research on the "advisor" and discovered this charlatan was not an authentic financial advisor—all he had was an insurance license. Jeff lost all his money in the fake deal, which was nearly $150,000.

I felt terrible for Jeff and still do, but I share this story often as a cautionary tale, hopeful to keep others from placing unearned trust in people whose only interest is stealing your money, under the guise of being a "financial advisor" when they couldn't be further from the title.

Now that you're aware of the drawbacks and downfalls of variable annuities, non-traded REITs, cash value life insurance, pump and dumps, and Ponzi schemes, it is my hope that you'll never blindly walk into one of these strategies and lose a lump sum of your hard-earned money. While it can be tempting when you're promised what appear to be reasonable—or even double-digit—returns on investment with these scams, remember that these fraudulent operators count on you *not* to perform due diligence on these offers, or to fall for being straight-out lied to.

Fortunately, by forging a trusted partnership with a true fiduciary, you will never be tempted, and certainly not strong-armed, into anything resembling these strategies to avoid. If you are presented with an opportunity outside of your advisory partnership that might sound prosperous, I recommend conferring with your financial advisor before agreeing to any investment. Chances are, your advisor is aware of the scheme, or can at least spot any red flags, and will steer you clear of what might have been a painful monetary loss.

In our next and final chapter, we'll discuss evaluating your portfolio, where you'll not only learn how to confirm your investments are doing well for you, but also that your fiduciary is truly aligned with your stated plans and goals.

8

EVALUATING PERFORMANCE:

Ensuring Your Partnership with Your Advisor Is Delivering Value

———•———

When you think about receiving value from having a financial advisor, your first thought probably jumps to whether or not you're seeing financial gain in your investments. This is definitely a critical component of your relationship—and we'll discuss how to evaluate that at length in this chapter—but there are other elements that contribute to the value of your partnership as well. In the sections that follow, we'll go over each of these so that you'll be equipped to assess the performance of your advisor within the four primary areas of what a fiduciary partnership should provide for you. If you're able to place a checkmark next to all or several components of each, meaning awareness and reasonable expectations are being fulfilled, you'll know your partnership is serving you well. If any area is lacking, you'll know where to place your focus in either improving performance with your financial advisor, or in re-evaluating if the partnership remains in your best interest.

1. AWARENESS AND DISCLOSURE OF FEES

As we discussed in Chapter 2, within a fee-only partnership you are either paying a **percentage-of-assets fee** or **assets under management (AUM) fee** (the most common within the fiduciary model), **a flat fee** (for one-time advice or yearly advice), or an **hourly fee** (least common). This should have been clear when you signed the agreement with your chosen financial advisor, and this should not change unless you mutually agree to alter your fee arrangement.

If you are with your advisor on an ongoing basis under an AUM or flat-fee agreement, these agreed-upon fees should be disclosed to you in a quarterly invoice. When you are aware of what fees you're paying for which services, you have the right to evaluate whether or not you're receiving value for your money. You can't make this assessment if you don't know what you're paying. What's more, advisors are much less likely to be complacent when clients are aware of the fees they're paying, and clients are much more likely to hold their advisor accountable for the work they're being paid to do on the client's behalf.

Now, I must note here that while a state-registered advisor managing less than $100 million in assets is required to send their clients a quarterly invoice detailing their charges, an advisor who manages over $100 million in assets—making them an SEC-registered firm—is no longer obligated to send their client that invoice. I personally believe every client should receive a quarterly invoice that shows the fees they are paying to their advisor—and I plan to continue doing so when we reach the level of becoming an SEC-registered firm. These fees should be disclosed in your investment statements (if your advisor is collecting their fee that way), but not all clients are knowledgeable enough to navigate the complex information that's provided. So do be aware of this dichotomy in the industry if you happen to have an advisor whose firm falls into the SEC-registered category.

Note also that if you're working with a broker for any reason outside of your fiduciary partnership, or with an insurance agent who is a broker, there is no disclosure required to detail what you're paying them. Statements frequently do not provide any indication of the fee you may be paying, or of any additional fees you're being charged for insurance products or commissions, so be sure you're not being taken in either of these relationships.

The **other fees** to be aware of would be any embedded costs inside your investment portfolio that are not disclosed on your quarterly statements. For example, if you're invested in mutual funds, you will be paying ongoing mutual fund costs, known as an expense ratio. You can easily look these up by going to www.morningstar.com and typing in your mutual fund symbol to see what the expense ratio is in your fund. You can also see the performance of that fund versus its comparable index. If you're unsure how to do this, you can ask your advisor to show you.

With all of this in mind, if you can answer yes to the following two statements, you can check off **Awareness of Costs** in your performance evaluation assessment:

- The fee arrangement with my advisor is straightforward, and the fees I am paying are clearly shown on a quarterly invoice and on my statements.
- The fees I'm paying within my investment portfolio are reasonable and known to me. (Reasonable is defined as

an average cost of less than .30 percent per year. If it exceeds that, the fees are too high and need to be lowered by altering your portfolio.)

2. PERFORMANCE OF INVESTMENT PORTFOLIO

As I said in the opening of the chapter, how well your investments are performing is not the only factor you should consider when evaluating your fiduciary partnership, but it's definitely a significant one. If you discover you're merely paying unnecessary fees, or that you're actually worse off than you were with no advisor, it may be a sign to leave the partnership. However, it's equally important to understand what reasonable investment performance may look like over time. While no financial advisor can guarantee how well your investments will perform, and markets consistently fluctuate, you should have a good idea of how well your portfolio is doing for you. To that end, we're going to examine multiple facets of evaluating your investment portfolio so that you're aware of all the angles to come from.

What You Can and Cannot Control

I can't overemphasize the importance of recognizing what you as an investor can and cannot control. Simply put:

+ You **cannot** control market conditions—and neither can your advisor
+ You **can** control how you and your advisor invest your money

✦ You **can** control your asset allocation strategy

✦ You **can** control your reaction to market volatility

The first two "**can control**" bullet points rely on you and your advisor working well together, and on your advisor's skills in his or her field. But the final bullet point is all about you. Here's what I mean.

The most competent advisor can provide sound counsel and offer the best advice, but you as a client must possess the inner fortitude to stay committed to your investment plan and avoid making hasty decisions at the wrong time. This requires a solid understanding of yourself, meaning you need to be aware of your natural response to risk and whether or not your tendency is to flee. If it is, it's critical to hang tight during a downturn, resist the urge to sell, and remain committed to long-term success, as a bailout will almost always result in harm to yourself.

Though I do recommend keeping an eye on your portfolio and reviewing your monthly or quarterly statements when they arrive, if you are a person who tends to be risk averse, you may want to avoid opening every statement and perusing your portfolio on a regular basis. I know this sounds counterintuitive, but if you know that seeing a drop in value will cause a visceral reaction that leads to stress and the urge to sell, it's better for you not to look. Think of it like closing your eyes on a roller coaster. Do you want to see the drop coming, or find out about it afterward?

Look, I get the conflict. On one hand, you should monitor your investments; on the other, you can shoot yourself in the foot by doing it too often. It certainly doesn't help that in the information age we live in, you can access statistics about your portfolio, through your phone and other devices, practically anytime. With this constant availability of information, you can easily drive yourself crazy during rough times because the market is outside your control—and what will eventually happen is that you'll feel compelled to do something to regain a sense of control, and that "something" is usually "I need to sell my portfolio."

Unfortunately, this is a sure-fire way, in almost all cases, to undermine your long-term success. You may feel like you've taken back control, but in reality, you've sacrificed your long-term goals for short-term relief. You must remember that the reason you're investing is to have a long-term plan as well as long-term success. When you sell, however, that's out the window.

This is why I always recommend that investors be mindful of the noise and distractions of the market and stay committed to their long-term investment goals. Short-term thinking and media hype may be alluring, but it can be detrimental to long-term financial success. The clients who have made the most money with me over the years have monitored their investments sparingly, stayed committed for the long haul, and trusted the process.

Having a Rebalancing Strategy

In Chapter 6, I touched briefly on rebalancing your asset allocation, but I want to expand on it a bit more here.

Every advisor should have a rebalancing strategy, and you should know what this strategy will be with regard to your portfolio to ensure it doesn't move out of alignment. For example:

Let's say your stock-to-bond ratio is 60/40, and that is the ratio we want to maintain. If your stock allocation increases from 60 percent to 65 percent, we'll sell some stock funds, and purchase bonds and cash, to get back to the 60/40 ratio. Conversely, if the allocation decreases to 55 percent stocks and 45 percent bonds, we'll sell some bonds and purchase stocks. This is how we manage rebalancing.

Although software and technology have made rebalancing easy to automate—and it can be set at a "trigger point" if the balance moves by 5 percent in either direction—in my firm we prefer to review portfolios individually to make these decisions. Yes, we use software to facilitate trading, but we don't rely on it to make investment decisions. Instead, we check each portfolio every quarter to see if rebalancing is required, and if so, make those decisions thoughtfully in the best interest of the client.

You will want to know how your advisor manages rebalancing, and how often. If you only have retirement accounts, automating the rebalancing makes sense. However, if you have taxable accounts as well, you probably don't want to automate it, as unnecessary taxes may be paid. The more complicated your portfolio is, the more you want to have your advisor oversee the rebalancing rather than have a computer do it. The reason this is important is twofold:

1. If a portfolio is not rebalanced, and over-concentration of stocks or other risky assets occurs, it could be detrimental in the event of a market decline. In other words, you will experience greater negative impact because you are carrying more risk.

2. If a portfolio is not rebalanced, and it becomes too conservative, you may not capture as much of the potential gain as you should during a bull market.

These two potential scenarios are why it's essential to manage both the upside and the downside, and why seeing if rebalancing is necessary on a quarterly basis, as is my recommendation.

Assessing Financial Gain

The easiest way to know if you're receiving financial gain is to see how your portfolio has performed versus a comparable benchmark. Here is an example:

> Let's say your portfolio is 100 percent in stocks. You could compare the performance of those stocks to the S&P 500. Over a year's time, if you find that your portfolio has averaged 6 percent when the S&P has averaged 3 percent, that's excellent. If the converse is true—your portfolio has averaged 3 percent when the S&P has averaged 6 percent—you know your portfolio is underperforming the benchmark, in which case your advisor should consider making some adjustments with you.
>
> However, the more diversified your portfolio becomes, meaning it includes both large-cap and small-cap stocks, as well as international stocks, the more customized your portfolio benchmark will need to become. You wouldn't want to compare your portfolio, for example, to the international stock market if it was purely invested in US-based stocks. In this case, your

advisor should be able to help you develop the right portfolio benchmarks.

As you begin to incorporate bonds into your portfolio, you will also need to adjust your benchmarks. If, for example, you're in a 60 percent stock and 40 percent bond portfolio, you wouldn't compare it to a 100 percent stock portfolio. In other words, you must be aware of what your portfolio allocation is and compare it to the correct overall portfolio benchmark. Your quarterly statements should help you determine your gains versus benchmarks, as well as accounting for fees. This is what we provide to clients in our firm, and I would hope your advisor does the same.

I must caution you that I have reviewed hundreds of portfolios for prospective clients, and I have many times found that these clients have been paying high fees over the years with a poor return compared to average benchmarks. Even though this was clear as day to me, the clients weren't aware of it. This is why, as a client, you must be certain you have a way to measure your portfolio's performance and that you are monitoring it. Your advisor should be providing you with performance reporting so you're clear on how you're doing versus benchmarks, but there *are* advisors who don't provide this, which I hate to say may be intentional. Let's be clear: **It should be very easy for you know how your portfolio is performing.** Unfortunately, there are many firms that don't want their clients to know how their portfolio is doing, precisely because the performance is poor. Yes, you can do some rough math and try to calculate your investment performance on your own, but not being given this information by your advisor is a red flag. Anyone who manages your money should have to provide performance reports against benchmarks—not only so that you know if you're earning gains or not, but also to ensure your advisor is doing the job they're being trusted and paid to do. If you're working with an advisor and the performance of your portfolio is terrible, you may want to think about hiring someone else.

In my firm, I pay for portfolio reporting software that allows our clients to log in to a website and view their performance at any time. This is a third-party website that ensures transparency for our clients. In other words, we're not influencing the information reported, so our clients know the data isn't being manipulated to show results that aren't true. They can choose whatever timeframe they wish to view, as far back as when we were hired to manage their portfolio. And, while it's nice to have this information available 24/7, I'll just offer a reminder here that if you're the client described earlier who tends to want to flee at the slightest dip, you'll definitely want to avoid logging in to a site like this too often, if indeed it's offered by your financial advisor.

Overall, you want your advisor to regularly ensure that your investment plan and portfolio is aligned with what's important to you, and that it is consistently delivering benefits, to the extent the market conditions allow at any given time.

If you can answer yes to the following five statements, you can check off **Performance of Investment Portfolio** in your performance evaluation assessment:

I'm aware of what I can and cannot control, and make sound decisions accordingly.

- I have a clear rebalancing strategy in place with my advisor, and he or she monitors it quarterly.

- The return on investment I'm receiving is in line with the appropriate benchmarks.

- The benchmarks I'm measuring are the correct ratios, based on the percentages of my portfolio that are invested in specific assets (such as 60 percent stocks, 40 percent mutual funds).

- I have a clear way of assessing these gains versus benchmarks, either through quarterly statements, an accessible website, or a report generated by my advisor's software that shows the appropriate comparisons.

3. FINANCIAL PLANNING BENEFITS

This third area can be challenging to measure, but if your advisor is assisting you with financial planning—retirement, insurance, taxes, and/or estate—you want to feel confident you're receiving value from the guidance. We explored each of these in detail in Chapter 5, but as a recap:

+ Do you have a financial plan that's aligned with your retirement goals, and is that plan being realized or moved forward?

+ Is your advisor helping you with your insurance policies to ensure you have the right coverage?

+ Does your advisor go over your taxes with you and help with tax planning?

+ Has your advisor helped devise a plan for your estate
  so that basic elements are covered, your wishes are in
  place, and the settlement will be simplified for your
  loved ones?
+ Has your advisor followed through with delivery to
  you of your financial plan?
+ Is your advisor updating your financial plan on a
  yearly basis?

Almost every financial advisor today claims to provide financial planning as part of their service; however, that term can be used loosely. I often find that advisors either don't follow through on delivering financial planning advice, or the advice is not actual financial planning but rather investment management. So do be certain that you can answer yes to the following four statements to check off **Financial Planning Benefits** in your performance evaluation assessment:

- **I have a written financial plan.**
- **My advisor goes over my financial plan annually and updates it with any changes in my life.**
- **My financial plan is comprehensive and includes retirement planning, investment management, tax planning, insurance planning, college planning, and estate planning.**
- **My advisor involves other professionals when necessary to help with my plan, such as attorneys, insurance agents, and accountants.**

4. COMMUNICATION

This final area is evaluating the communication within the relationship with your advisor. Some questions to ask are:

+ Do you hear from your advisor at least once a year, to find out if there have been any major life changes that have occurred for you that would warrant taking a deeper dive into your financial plan and your portfolio?

+ How does your advisor stay in contact with you? Via email, phone calls, Zoom meetings, in-person meetings? Is the method amenable to you?

+ If you reach out to your advisor with updates or questions, does he or she make time to discuss your needs, as well as follow up on requests?

+ Is your advisor coordinating with your other advisors, if applicable (accountant, attorney, insurance agent, stockbroker) to ensure they're working as a team and not missing any opportunities for you?

+ When you meet with your advisor to review your portfolio: Do you discuss spending habits, such as spending more than your portfolio can mathematically accommodate, or spending less than you could, to maintain an appropriate balance?

+ Do you look over what you own in your portfolio?

+ Do you get clarification on fees, if necessary?

+ Is your advisor proactive about making adjustments based on life changes or revised goals?

If these elements are present in your communication with your advisor, you should feel good about this area of your partnership. If any of these are lacking, it may simply involve bringing a concern to your advisor's attention. Don't assume your advisor knows everything you need. Give them an opportunity to make things better instead of getting upset or filing a complaint. If things still don't improve after voicing your concerns, it may be a sign to seek a new financial advisor.

In my firm, for example, anytime a client needs something, they're free to reach out to us via phone or email, and we do our best to respond in a timely manner. We also do a substantial amount of analysis for clients on their portfolios, their taxes, and their financial plan. If we see an issue, we'll reach out to them. If not, we'll go over any concerns or suggested changes in our biannual scheduled meetings. In this way, we strive to overdeliver in the area of communication, contributing to the value our clients receive for what they're paying.

One last thing your advisor should stay on top of with regard to communication is your age. When people near 50, for example, they tend to become more serious about planning for retirement. At 59 and a half, you can potentially take money out of your retirement accounts without a penalty. Turning 62 means potentially collecting Social Security; at 65, you can start collecting Medicare. Finally, at 73, you have to start taking money out of retirement accounts. Whether you are aware and bring this to your advisor's attention, or your advisor notes it and brings it up to you in your meetings, conversations around these milestones should occur within your partnership, preferably a year or so before the age arrives. For example:

Before a biannual meeting, I always check what my client's age is. I also have software that contains the birthdays of all my clients. When I see that someone is going to be turning 50 next year, I'll reach out (if we haven't already discussed it in a prior meeting) and ask if they want to increase their retirement plan contributions. The same is true for the other ages listed prior.

If you can answer yes to the following four statements, you can check off **Communication** in your performance evaluation assessment:

- I hear from my advisor at least once a year, via a method that's comfortable for me.

- When I reach out for advice, or communicate any relevant changes, my advisor responds or acts on those changes in a timely manner.

- If I have other members of my financial team, my advisor works with them to ensure I have a solid plan and that I'm not missing important opportunities.

- During annual or biannual meetings, my advisor discusses pertinent information with me, such as my asset allocation, clarification on fees, reaching a milestone age with regard to retirement and benefits, updating my financial plan, spending and saving habits, if applicable, and my plan for the following year.

In summary, you should feel confident that all four categories are fulfilled by your fiduciary partnership: 1) awareness and disclosure of fees; 2) performance of investment portfolio; 3) financial planning benefits (if they apply); and 4) communication. If you were able to check all, or the majority, of the boxes at the end of each section, you should feel great about the value you're receiving for the fees you're investing in working with your financial advisor. If anything is lacking, it is my hope that the guidance in this book will help you get on track as a team.

As I tell our clients, "We are here to add value to your situation by advising you, helping you to plan for your goals while minimizing taxes, and improving your portfolio." If, however, a client expresses that what we're doing is *not* adding value, and there doesn't seem to be a way of rectifying that, I'm honest and tell them they shouldn't pay us anymore, and that they should probably take their account to another firm. I don't say this to encourage clients to leave, as my goal is always to make a relationship right if at all possible; perhaps there's miscommunication we can improve upon. However, if you've given fair assessment to the partnership you have with your financial advisor using the checklists in this chapter, and you don't find their services viable, you shouldn't continue to pay for those services. You don't want to compromise on something as substantial as investing your money for your future, or on sound financial planning, so it is your right as a client to seek another partnership if your current one isn't truly serving your best interest.

When the partnership is serving you well, however, and you witness consistent growth of your assets, pay fair fees in achieving that growth, and enjoy communication that is respectful and supportive, it is my sincere hope that you will remain in the relationship with your fiduciary and that it will be long and prosperous.

C

CONCLUSION

———○———

I f you came to this book with little to no knowledge about finding, hiring, and establishing an aligned and trusted partnership with a financial advisor, or if a previous relationship with an advisor was less than favorable and you were hesitant to enter into another one, I hope the chapters in this book have given you all you need to know to forge a partnership that will be lasting and beneficial to you.

Is the industry flawed? Yes. Do advisors and brokers act unethically in some cases? Yes. As someone who takes ethics seriously in my field, this bothers me a great deal. This is why I believe all financial advisors should be fiduciaries and adhere to the fiduciary oath, and why I wrote this book: to guide people like you toward the most ethical arrangement when it comes to trusting someone to invest and advise you with your money.

I, as much as you, believe the field of financial advising must hold fast to guiding principles that are embodied in daily practice. Only in implementing them can we create a trustworthy system that serves the interests of you as a client and fosters the credence that is essential to this industry. If the regulatory body required all financial advisors to be fee-only, and broker-dealers to solely be brokers, it would most certainly improve competency levels and elevate our profession.

A few years ago, Australia outlawed all commissions paid from investment products to financial advisors and brokers—and many advisors are pushing for these changes in the US as well: requiring financial advisors to be fee-only and have a Certified Financial Planning designation. Unfortunately, we face resistance from Wall Street, which prioritizes commissions and fees over clients' interests, making it challenging to achieve reform. This is, in part, because many of the regulators making the rules are former Wall Street executives.

Despite these flaws in the system, however, there are thousands of ethical fiduciaries who run their firms with the standards laid out in this book. And now that you have the essential attributes, questions, and evaluation tools to empower you in finding your ideal advisor, you can take action—and take control—of your financial future. I've worked with so many clients who never considered planning for retirement, or having a solid financial plan, until they received a harsh wakeup call: the loss of a high school friend or acquaintance, an unexpected career change, or even retirement age sneaking up on them. Any of these can be a prompt to get serious about ensuring your family will be financially secure if something were to happen to you. But rather than wait until a pivotal moment occurs, or allow procrastination to be a hindrance, I encourage you to use this book to act now instead of relying on unpredictable events before you take action.

I hope the preceding chapters have demonstrated that working with a financial advisor to save and invest for retirement doesn't have to be scary, intimidating, or complicated. I know it can induce anxiety to think of letting someone else manage your investment strategies, but think of it the same way you would hire a professional to perform any task that's not within your own expertise. If you know nothing about plumbing or electrical wiring, or it might be dangerous to go DIY, you'd hire a plumber or an electrician; if landscaping isn't a talent you possess, you'd hire someone who does have that talent. The list goes on.

Even in areas where you might be naturally gifted or able to learn easily and can swing the do-it-yourself route, managing money and navigating appropriate investment strategies is a complex arena. This is why I recommend seeking expert guidance from an ethical fiduciary: we put thousands of hours into gaining and maintaining credentials and expertise in our field, precisely so that we can take anxiety away from you, manage your assets efficiently, and give you peace of mind.

And if you want to take it a step further, I highly encourage you to impart this same advice to your children. The sooner you introduce the benefits of a solid financial plan and investment strategy, the better off your children will be in the long run. If they learn to seek advice from an expert—based on the guidance in this book—on establishing a sound financial foundation, they will be more likely to avoid falling prey to sales pitches and other questionable practices employed by brokers, as well as making poor money decisions that could be detrimental to them later in life.

I also want to remind you that while the arena of finance may be complex, you don't have to hit home runs to be successful as an investor; singles and doubles can grow your assets or allow you to remain wealthy. Exotic investments and complex strategies may sound great, but when you look at the long term, they often perform poorly and lose money for investors. By sticking with some of the basic investments in stocks, bonds, and cash outlined in this book, guided by your fiduciary, you are likely to experience lower risk and greater gain—and that steady growth is what gives you peace of mind as you look ahead to your future.

From the time I established my independent practice, my goal has been to deliver financial nirvana to my clients. Using the standards set forth in this book, I hope the fiduciary you ultimately decide to hire strives for and delivers the same to you.

CONNECT WITH RYAN

Sign up for the weekly *Retire with Ryan* podcast and free Retirement Readiness newsletter, which includes helpful tips, articles, and early access to courses and workshops, delivered to your inbox each week. As a gift for signing up, you'll also receive my Retirement Ready Tool Kit, a downloadable PDF to help you organize your budget and retirement plan.

www.retirewithryan.com/newsletter

OR

Scan the QR code below:

ABOUT THE AUTHOR

RYAN R. MORRISSEY is a financial advisor and president of Morrissey Wealth Management in North Haven, Connecticut. He specializes in helping people over fifty develop and implement a plan for retirement. He is also the host of the podcast, *Retire with Ryan*, and is a public speaker and educator. He has earned the designations of CERTIFIED FINANCIAL PLANNER™, Chartered Financial Consultant®, Chartered Life Underwriter®, and Chartered Mutual Fund Counselor®. These sought-after designations required advanced coursework in taxes, retirement planning, estate planning, investments, and risk management. Maintaining these designations demands a rigorous program of ongoing education and adherence to a strict code of ethics, which he is proud to uphold.

Ryan lives in Cheshire, Connecticut, with his wife Tiffany, son Ryan Jr., and daughter Emilia. He is an avid golfer and enjoys spending time with family, attending UConn sporting events, and further educating himself about his profession. Find out more at www.retirewithryan.com.

www.ingramcontent.com/pod-product-compliance
Lightning Source LLC
Chambersburg PA
CBHW030509210326
41597CB00013B/850